GIFTS GALORE IN PLASTIC CANVAS

When you give a handmade gift, you share the greatest gift of all — a piece of your heart. This treasury of gifts to make offers ideas for every occasion, from birthdays and weddings to personal moments such as telling a friend who's moving, "Let's keep in touch." We've also included lots of quick-and-easy pieces because we know you're often short on time. For whatever reason you need a gift — even for no reason at all — you'll discover the perfect present in Gifts Galore!

LEISURE ARTS, INC.
and
OXMOOR HOUSE, INC.

GIFTS GALORE IN PLASTIC CANVAS

EDITORIAL STAFF

Editor-in-Chief: Anne Van Wagner Childs
Executive Director: Sandra Graham Case
Executive Editor: Susan Frantz Wiles
Publications Director: Carla Bentley
Creative Art Director: Gloria Bearden
Production Art Director: Melinda Stout

PRODUCTION
Managing Editor: Teal Lee Elliott
Project Coordinators: Michelle Sass Goodrich, Catherine Hubmann, Susan McManus Johnson, and Rhonda Goerke Lombardo

EDITORIAL
Associate Editor: Linda L. Trimble
Senior Editorial Writer: Tammi Williamson Bradley
Editorial Writers: Jonathon Walker and Terri Leming Davidson
Copy Editor: Laura Lee Weland

DESIGN
Design Director: Patricia Wallenfang Sowers

ART
Crafts Art Director: Rhonda Hodge Shelby
Senior Production Artist: Jonathan M. Flaxman
Production Artists: Roberta Aulwes, Sonya McFatrich, Katie Murphy, Dana Vaughn, and Karen L. Wilson
Photography Stylists: Charlisa Erwin Parker, Sondra Daniel, Wanda Young, Aurora Huston, and Laura Bushmiaer

ADVERTISING AND DIRECT MAIL
Senior Editor: Tena Kelley Vaughn
Copywriters: Steven M. Cooper and Marla Shivers
Designer: Rhonda H. Hestir
Art Director: Jeff Curtis
Production Artists: Linda Lovette Smart and Angie Griffin

BUSINESS STAFF

Publisher: Steve Patterson
Controller: Tom Siebenmorgen
Retail Sales Director: Richard Tignor
Retail Marketing Director: Pam Stebbins
Retail Customer Services Director: Margaret Sweetin
Marketing Manager: Russ Barnett

Executive Director of Marketing and Circulation: Guy A. Crossley
Fulfillment Manager: Byron L. Taylor
Print Production Manager: Laura Lockhart
Print Production Coordinator: Nancy Reddick Lister

GIFTS GALORE IN PLASTIC CANVAS
from the *Plastic Canvas Creations* series
Published by Leisure Arts, Inc., and Oxmoor House, Inc.

Library of Congress Catalog Number 94-77912
Hardcover: 0-942237-53-6
Softcover: 0-942237-52-8

TABLE OF CONTENTS

PLANTER COVER

Skill Level: Beginner

Size: 3"h x 4¼" dia

Supplies: Worsted weight yarn (refer to color key), one 10½" x 13½" sheet of 10 mesh plastic canvas, #20 tapestry needle, and 3"h x 4" dia planter

Stitches Used: Gobelin Stitch, Overcast Stitch, and Tent Stitch

Instructions: For Side, cut a piece of plastic canvas 123 x 29 threads. Follow chart and use required stitches to work Side, repeating charted pattern until piece is completely worked. Use yarn color to match stitching area to join unworked edges, forming a cylinder. Slide Planter Cover over planter.

Planter Cover designed by Ann Townsend.

white - 13 yds

pink - 18 yds

dk pink - 3 yds

blue - 6 yds

dk blue - 5 yds

green - 4 yds

Side (123 x 29 threads)

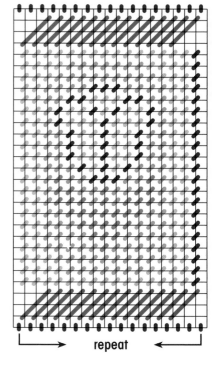

repeat

4

DOORSTOP DOGGIE

Delight a dog owner with this cute canine doorstop! Ever ready to guard against unwanted closings, he's crafted using a variety of stitches and weighted with a brick. For added appeal, we collared our furry friend with a bright red bow and a jingle bell. The doggie biscuit is stitched separately and then attached for a tasty finishing touch.

5

DOG DOORSTOP

Skill Level: Intermediate

Size: 7½"w x 13½"h x 5¼"d

(**Note:** Fits a 3⅝"w x 8"h x 2⅛"d brick.)

Supplies: Worsted weight yarn or Needloft® Plastic Canvas Yarn (refer to color key), three 10½" x 13½" sheets of 7 mesh plastic canvas, #16 tapestry needle, 24" of 1"w red satin ribbon, ½" gold jingle bell, two 15mm brown shank animal eyes, one 25mm black shank animal nose, plastic wrap, brick, nylon line, #26 tapestry needle (for working with nylon line), a fine-toothed comb, and clear-drying craft glue

Stitches Used: Backstitch, Fringe, Gobelin Stitch, Overcast Stitch, and Tent Stitch

Instructions: Follow charts and use required stitches to work Dog Doorstop pieces. Complete backgrounds with grey Tent Stitches as indicated on charts. For Back, cut a piece of plastic canvas 26 x 53 threads. Work Back with grey Tent Stitches. Insert eyes through openings in Front and glue in place. With right sides up, use white and match ✗'s to tack Muzzle Bottom to wrong side of Muzzle between ✗'s. Use white and match ▲'s to join Muzzle Side to wrong side of Muzzle. Insert nose through opening in Muzzle and glue in place. Refer to photo and use white to tack Muzzle Side to Front. Use grey to join Short Sides to Long Sides along short edges. Use white to join one Short Side to Front along unworked edge. Use nylon line to securely tack remaining Sides to Front. Wrap brick with plastic wrap and insert into Doorstop. Use grey to join Back to Sides. Use tan to join Bone pieces. Refer to photo to glue Bone to Front. Refer to photo to comb Fringe. Trim Fringe for eyebrows to ½". Trim Fringe for beard to 2½". Refer to photo to shape combed Fringe. Refer to photo to tie ribbon in a bow around Front. Use nylon line to sew jingle bell to bow.

Dog Doorstop designed by Victor Espinoza.

Long Side (18 x 53 threads) (Work 2)

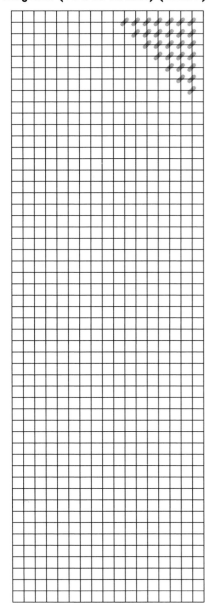

Muzzle Side (5 x 41 threads)

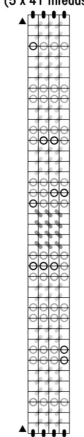

Short Side (26 x 18 threads) (Work 2)

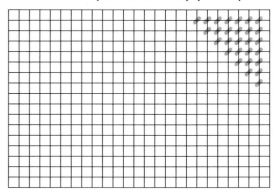

Bone (29 x 11 threads) (Work 2)

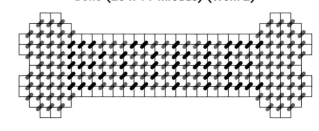

Muzzle (22 x 15 threads)

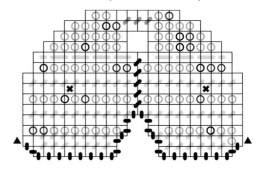

Muzzle Bottom (15 x 8 threads)

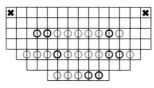

NL	COLOR	
00	black	2 yds
07	pink	4 yds
14	brown	2 yds
16	tan	4 yds
37	lt grey	23 yds
38	grey	90 yds
41	white	43 yds
41	white	2 strands
00	black Fringe	4 yds
37	lt grey Fringe	8 yds
38	grey Fringe	6 yds
41	white Fringe	53 yds

Front (48 x 89 threads)

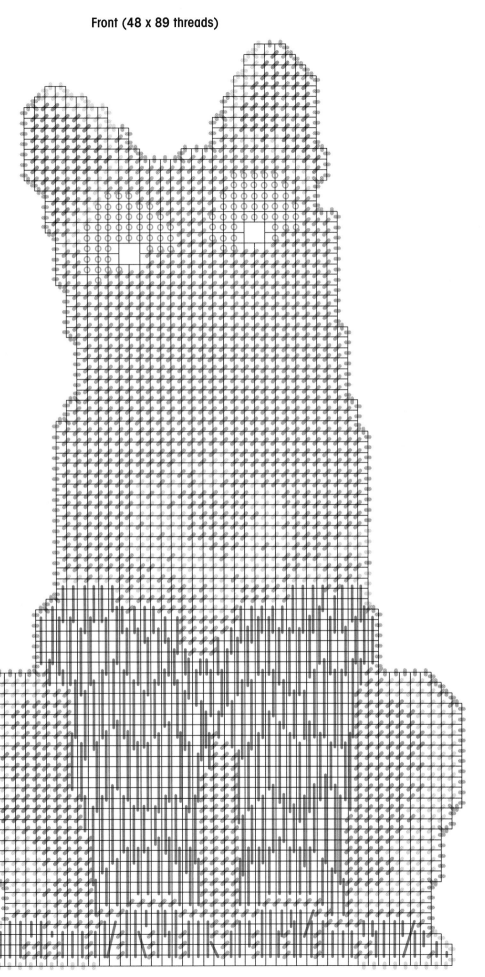

BABY'S HERE!

Help the proud parents announce baby's arrival with this charming door decoration! It's perfect for the nursery, the front door, or even Mom's hospital room. For a baby girl, simply change the message, stitch the border in pink, and give the teddy a pretty pink bow.

NEW BABY DOOR DECORATION

Skill Level: Intermediate
Size: 17³/₄"w x 12¹/₂"h
Supplies: Worsted weight yarn or Needloft® Plastic Canvas Yarn (refer to color key), one 13⁵/₈" x 21⁵/₈" sheet of 5 mesh plastic canvas, #16 tapestry needle, sawtooth hanger, 8" length of ³/₈"w satin ribbon, and clear-drying craft glue or hot glue gun and glue sticks
Stitches Used: Backstitch, Overcast Stitch, and Tent Stitch
Instructions: Use two strands of yarn for all stitches, unless otherwise indicated in color key. (**Note:** Checkerboard and words may be stitched in pink or blue.) Follow chart and use required stitches to work New Baby Door Decoration. Complete background with white Tent Stitches, leaving shaded area unworked. Follow Boy Chart or Girl Chart to work shaded area, completing background with white Tent Stitches. Tie ribbon in a bow and trim ends. Refer to photo to glue bow to bear. For hanger, glue sawtooth hanger to wrong side of stitched piece.

New Baby Door Decoration designed by Maryanne Moreck.

NL	COLOR		NL	COLOR
00	black - 2 yds		35	lt blue - 28 yds
00	black - 1 strand		40	lt brown - 11 yds
07	lt pink - 15 yds		41	white - 88 yds
14	dk brown - 4 yds		43	brown - 22 yds
17	gold - 7 yds		55	pink - 15 yds
27	green - 22 yds		57	lt gold - 13 yds
32	blue - 27 yds			

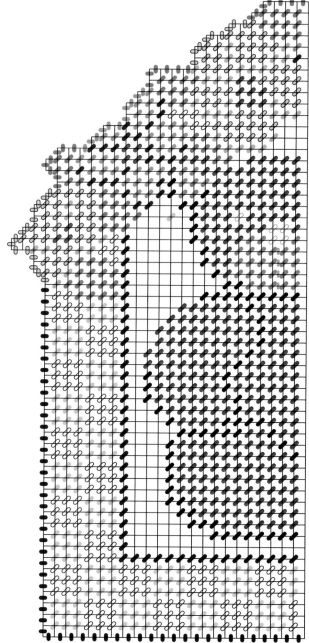

Boy Chart

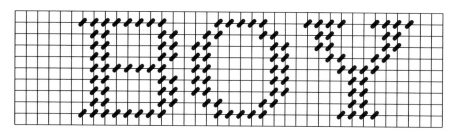

Girl Chart

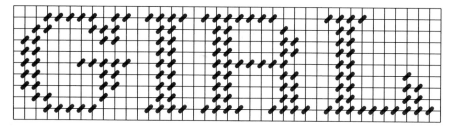

Door Decoration (89 x 63 threads)

Patriotic Luggage Tags

Sporting the flags of the United States or Canada, these patriotic luggage tags are just the ticket to wish your traveling friends Bon Voyage! *Each tag has an opening on one side to display identification information, and a beaded chain makes it easy to attach to a luggage handle.*

LUGGAGE TAGS
Skill Level: Beginner
Size: 3⁵/₈"w x 2¹/₄"h
Supplies: Needloft® Plastic Canvas Yarn or worsted weight yarn (refer to color key), one 10¹/₂" x 13¹/₂" sheet of 7 mesh plastic canvas, #16 tapestry needle, and bead chain key ring
Stitches Used: Backstitch, French Knot, Overcast Stitch, and Tent Stitch
Instructions: Follow charts and use required stitches to work Luggage Tag pieces. Use gold to join Front to Back along unworked edges. Refer to photo to attach bead chain key ring to Luggage Tag.

Luggage Tags designed by Diane Villano.

NL	COLOR
02	Christmas red
17	gold
32	royal
41	white
41	white 1-ply Fr. Knot

United States Front (24 x 15 threads)

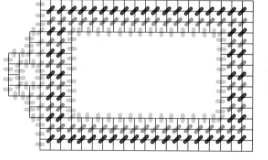

United States Back (24 x 15 threads)

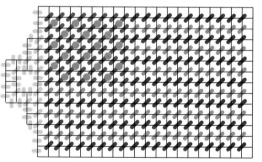

Canada Front (24 x 15 threads)

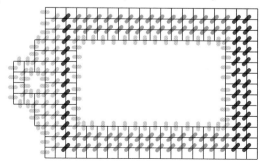

Canada Back (24 x 15 threads)

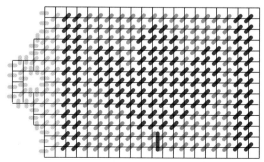

Charming Birdhouse

For a gift that's sure to please a bird-watching friend, this ingenious decorative birdhouse is top-flight! A charming way to bring a bit of nature indoors, it's trimmed with pretty flowers and a tiny bird.

BIRDHOUSE

Skill Level: Beginner

Size: 8½"w x 7"h x 8"d

Supplies: Worsted weight yarn or Needloft® Plastic Canvas Yarn (refer to color key), three 10½" x 13½" sheets of 7 mesh plastic canvas, #16 tapestry needle, 36" of ¼"w braided jute ribbon, five 14" lengths of satin ribbon (refer to photo), silk flowers, lightweight artificial bird, 2½" long twig or dowel for perch, and clear-drying craft glue or hot glue gun and glue sticks

Stitches Used: Backstitch, Gobelin Stitch, Overcast Stitch, Scotch Stitch, and Tent Stitch

Instructions: Follow charts and use required stitches to work Birdhouse pieces.

For Back, work Front, completing Scotch Stitch pattern and omitting brown stitches in center. Use lt brown to join Sides along long unworked edges. Use lt brown to join Front and Back to Sides. Use brown to join Roof pieces along unworked edges. Refer to photo and use brown to tack Roof to Front, Back, and Sides. Refer to photo to glue perch to Front. Refer to photo to glue bird to perch. Refer to photo to glue jute ribbon to Roof. Refer to photo to glue flowers to Birdhouse. Refer to photo to tie ribbon lengths together in a bow. Refer to photo to glue bow to flowers.

Birdhouse designed by Dolores Faihst.

NL	COLOR	
	13	brown - 98 yds
	13	brown - 2 strands
	16	lt brown - 87 yds

Roof (54 x 40 threads) (Work 2)

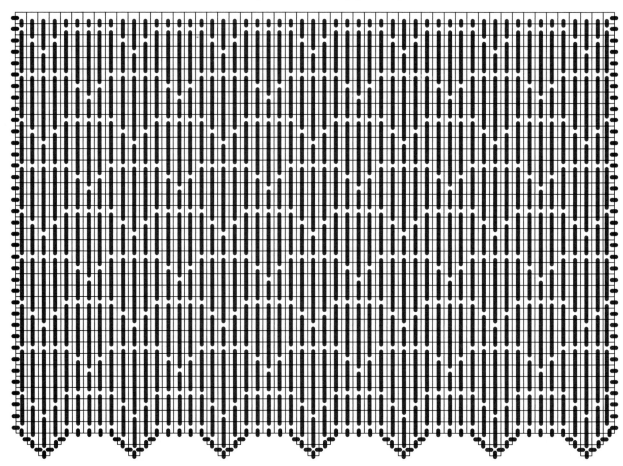

Side (38 x 32 threads) (Work 2)

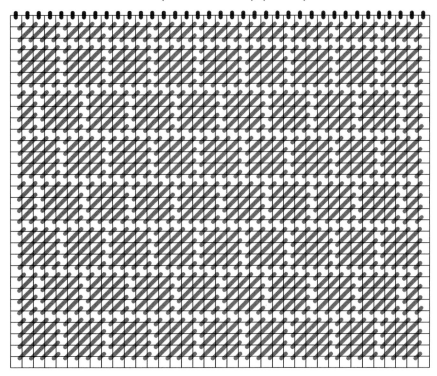

Front/Back (44 x 44 threads) (Cut 2, Work 1)

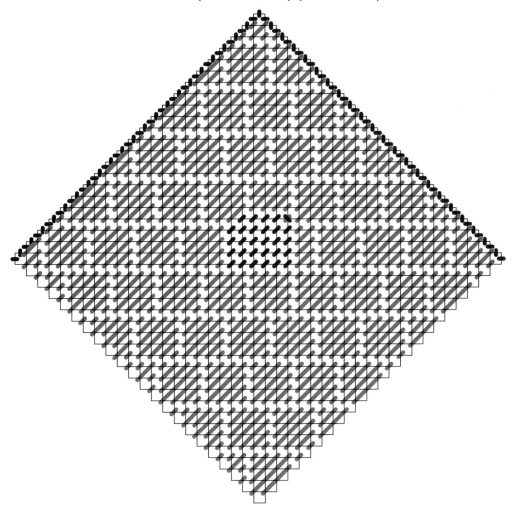

Fanciful Tooth Fairy

This fanciful doll will delight a little one who's expecting a visit from the Tooth Fairy! Accented with metallic silver, the curly-haired miss has a handy pouch for holding a baby tooth — and later for keeping the money that's left in its place.

TOOTH FAIRY

Skill Level: Intermediate

Size: 8"w x 10½"h

Supplies: Worsted weight yarn or Needloft® Plastic Canvas Yarn (refer to color key), metallic silver yarn, two 10½" x 13½" sheets of 7 mesh plastic canvas, #16 tapestry needle, curly blonde doll hair, 7" of 96"w white tulle, VELCRO® brand fastening tape, sewing needle, white thread, clear-drying craft glue

Stitches Used: Alternating Scotch Stitch, Backstitch, Cross Stitch, Gobelin Stitch, Overcast Stitch, and Tent Stitch

Instructions: Follow charts and use required stitches to work Tooth Fairy pieces. For hanger, thread 24" of pink yarn through Body Back at *'s. Tie yarn in a knot on wrong side of Body Back. Use yarn to match stitching area for all joining. With right sides together, match ▲'s to join Wing A to Body Back. With right sides together, match ◆'s to join Wing B to Body Back. Join Lower Leg Fronts to Lower Leg Backs, leaving area between ◆'s open. Join Upper Legs together along side edges. Match ◆'s to join Upper Legs to Lower Legs. Join Arm A pieces to Arm B pieces, leaving area between ♠'s open. With wrong sides together, place Body Front on Body Back. Refer to photo and match ♠'s to join Arms to Body Front and Body Back. Match ◆'s to join Upper Legs to Body Front and Body Back. Join Body Front to Body Back along remaining unworked edges. Refer to photo and follow manufacturer's instructions to glue hair to Body Front and Body Back. Cut a 9" length of dk pink yarn. Tie yarn in a bow and trim ends. Glue bow to hair. Cut four 9" lengths of metallic silver yarn. Tie three lengths of metallic yarn into bows and trim ends. Refer to photo to glue bows to Body Front and Lower Leg Fronts. For tutu, fold tulle in half lengthwise. Use sewing needle and a double thickness of thread to baste long edges together ¼" from edges. Gather tulle to measure 5". Refer to photo to place tutu around Body; tie ends of basting threads together to secure. For Pouch, join Pouch Front to Pouch Side. Join Pouch Side to Pouch Back along unworked edges. Glue Tooth to Pouch Front. For closure, sew VELCRO® fastening tape to Pouch Front and wrong side of Pouch Back. Refer to photo to place remaining metallic yarn length around neck and under Arm. Glue metallic yarn ends to Pouch Side.

Tooth Fairy designed by Jack Peatman for LuvLee Designs.

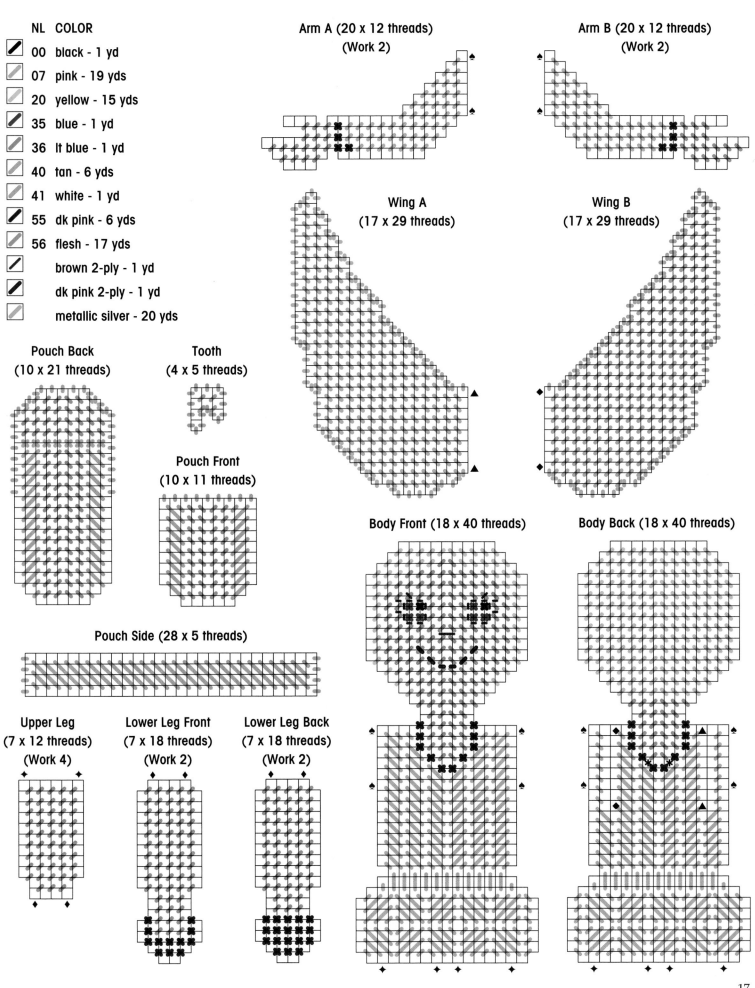

NL COLOR
00 black - 1 yd
07 pink - 19 yds
20 yellow - 15 yds
35 blue - 1 yd
36 lt blue - 1 yd
40 tan - 6 yds
41 white - 1 yd
55 dk pink - 6 yds
56 flesh - 17 yds
   brown 2-ply - 1 yd
   dk pink 2-ply - 1 yd
   metallic silver - 20 yds

Arm A (20 x 12 threads)
(Work 2)

Arm B (20 x 12 threads)
(Work 2)

Wing A
(17 x 29 threads)

Wing B
(17 x 29 threads)

Pouch Back
(10 x 21 threads)

Tooth
(4 x 5 threads)

Pouch Front
(10 x 11 threads)

Pouch Side (28 x 5 threads)

Upper Leg
(7 x 12 threads)
(Work 4)

Lower Leg Front
(7 x 18 threads)
(Work 2)

Lower Leg Back
(7 x 18 threads)
(Work 2)

Body Front (18 x 40 threads)

Body Back (18 x 40 threads)

COUNTRY PIG COASTERS

Here's a fun surprise for someone who's a real "ham" about displaying country collectibles! The cute coasters will add a whimsical touch to any decor, as well as protect surfaces from unsightly water rings. Stored in a pigpen holder, these little piggies are sure to cause a chuckle whenever they're used.

COASTER SET

Skill Level: Beginner
Coaster Size: 4¹/₄"w x 4¹/₄"h
Holder Size: 4¹/₂"w x 2"h x 2¹/₄"d
Supplies: Worsted weight yarn or Needloft® Plastic Canvas Yarn (refer to color key), two 10¹/₂" x 13¹/₂" sheets of 7 mesh plastic canvas, #16 tapestry needle, cork or felt, and clear-drying craft glue
Stitches Used: Backstitch, French Knot, Gobelin Stitch, Overcast Stitch, and Tent Stitch
Instructions: Follow charts and use required stitches to work Coaster Set pieces. Refer to photo and use ecru to join Front and Back to Sides. Use green to join Bottom to Front, Back, and Sides. For each tail, cut an 8" length of peach yarn. Secure yarn on wrong side of Coaster. Bring loose end of yarn up at ▲. Tie yarn in a loose knot close to Coaster. Secure yarn on wrong side of Coaster. For backing, cut cork or felt slightly smaller than Coaster and glue to wrong side of stitched piece.

Coaster Set designed by Toni Erwin.

NL	COLOR
✏ 00	black - 5 yds
✏ 01	red - 22 yds
✏ 28	green - 8 yds
✏ 33	blue - 2 yds
✏ 39	ecru - 12 yds
✏ 47	peach - 43 yds
✏ 55	dk peach - 1 yd
● 00	black Fr. Knot

Coaster (28 x 28 threads) (Work 6)

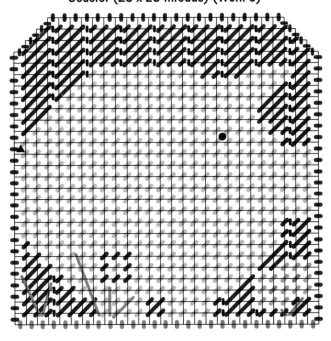

Bottom (30 x 14 threads)

Front/Back (30 x 13 threads) (Work 2)

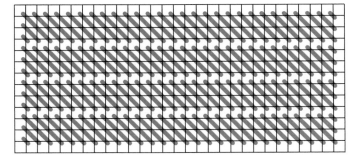

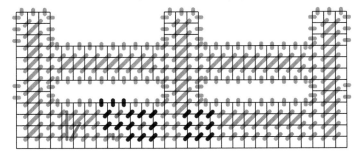

Side (14 x 13 threads) (Work 2)

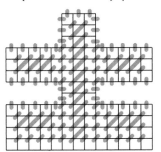

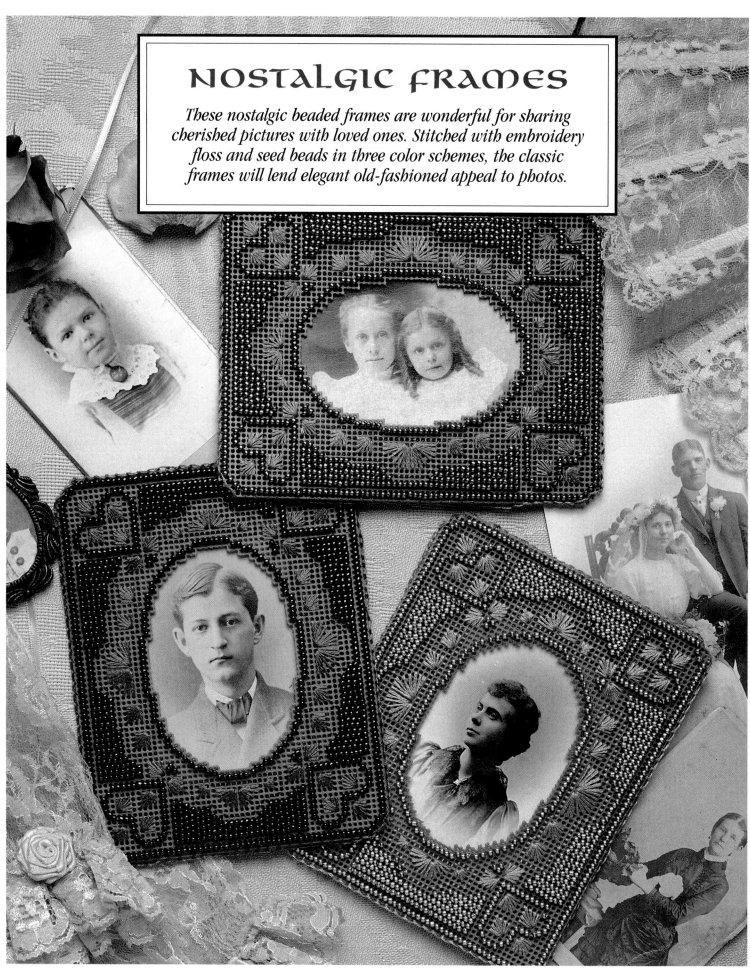

NOSTALGIC FRAMES

These nostalgic beaded frames are wonderful for sharing cherished pictures with loved ones. Stitched with embroidery floss and seed beads in three color schemes, the classic frames will lend elegant old-fashioned appeal to photos.

BEADED FRAMES

Skill Level: Intermediate
Size: 4⅛"w x 5¼"h
Opening Size: 2"w x 3"h
Supplies: Eight yards of DMC embroidery floss (356, 926, or 3773), one 8¼" x 11" sheet of brown 14 mesh perforated plastic, five 2.25g packages of Mill Hill Antique Glass Beads (03038, 03037, or 03039), #24 tapestry needle, and beading needle

Stitches Used: Backstitch, Beaded Tent Stitch, Blanket Stitch, and Gobelin Stitch
Instructions: Follow chart and use 2 strands of floss to work Backstitches. Follow chart and use 3 strands of floss to work Gobelin Stitches. Follow chart and use 1 strand of floss to work Beaded Tent Stitches. Use 2 strands of floss to work Blanket Stitches along top edge of Front. For Back, cut a piece of perforated plastic the same as Front without opening.

Work Blanket Stitch to join Front to Back along unworked edges of Front.

Beaded Frames designed by Kathy Elrod.

| ⟋ | DMC embroidery floss |
| ⟋ | Mill Hill Antique Glass Beads |

Front (57 x 73 threads)

These cute gift bags are great for disguising hard-to-wrap items! The white canvas makes a nice background that doesn't need stitching, so the totes are fast to finish for your last-minute gifts. The recipient can enjoy them again later by "recycling" the bags to present other gifts!

GIFT BAGS

Skill Level: Beginner

Size: 5"w x 6½"h x 2¾"d

Supplies: Worsted weight yarn or Needloft® Plastic Canvas Yarn (refer to color key), two 10½" x 13½" sheets of white 7 mesh plastic canvas, and #16 tapestry needle

Stitches Used: Alternating Overcast Stitch, Backstitch, French Knot, and Tent Stitch

Instructions: Refer to photo for design placement. Follow chart and use required stitches to work desired motif on Front. For Sides, cut two pieces of plastic canvas 18 x 43 threads each. Use Alternating Overcast Stitches with desired yarn color for all joining. Join Front and Back to Sides along long edges. For Bottom, cut a piece of plastic canvas 33 x 18 threads. Join Bottom to Front, Back, and Sides. For each handle, cut nine 24" lengths of yarn. Knot yarn lengths together 2" from one end. Thread long loose yarn ends through right side of Front at ★. Refer to photo to braid yarn to desired handle length. Thread ends of yarn through wrong side of Front at ✦. Knot yarn on right side of Front and trim ends. Repeat for remaining handle on Back.

Ladybug Motif

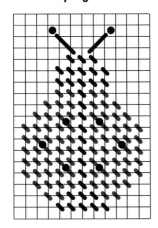

NL	COLOR	
✎	00	black
✎	02	red
✎	57	gold
●	00	black Fr. Knot

Scottie Motif

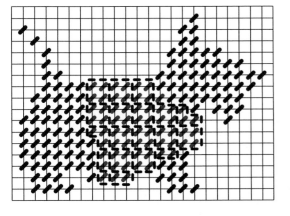

Argyle Motif

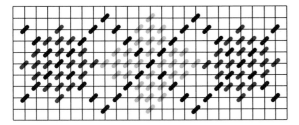

Front/Back (33 x 43 threads) (Cut 2)

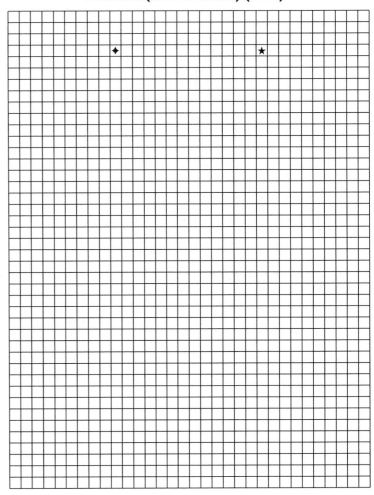

DELIGHTFUL DAISIES

*Delight a friend with this daisy boutique tissue box cover.
Its bright colors and cheerful basket design will lend an airy
feel to the bath — or any room — all through the year!*

DAISY BASKET TISSUE BOX COVER

Skill Level: Intermediate
Size: 4½"w x 5½"h x 4½"d
(**Note:** Fits a 4¼"w x 5¼"h x 4¼"d boutique tissue box.)
Supplies: Worsted weight yarn or Needloft® Plastic Canvas Yarn (refer to color key), two 10½" x 13½" sheets of 7 mesh plastic canvas, and #16 tapestry needle
Stitches Used: Backstitch, French Knot, Gobelin Stitch, Overcast Stitch, and Tent Stitch
Instructions: Follow charts and use required stitches to work Daisy Basket Tissue Box Cover pieces. Refer to photo for yarn color used for joining. Join Sides along long edges. Join Top to Sides.

Daisy Basket Tissue Box Cover designed by Dick Martin.

NL	COLOR
✎ 13	brown - 27 yds
✎ 23	green - 23 yds
✎ 41	white - 2 strands - 23 yds
✎ 57	yellow - 3 yds
◉ 57	yellow Fr. Knot

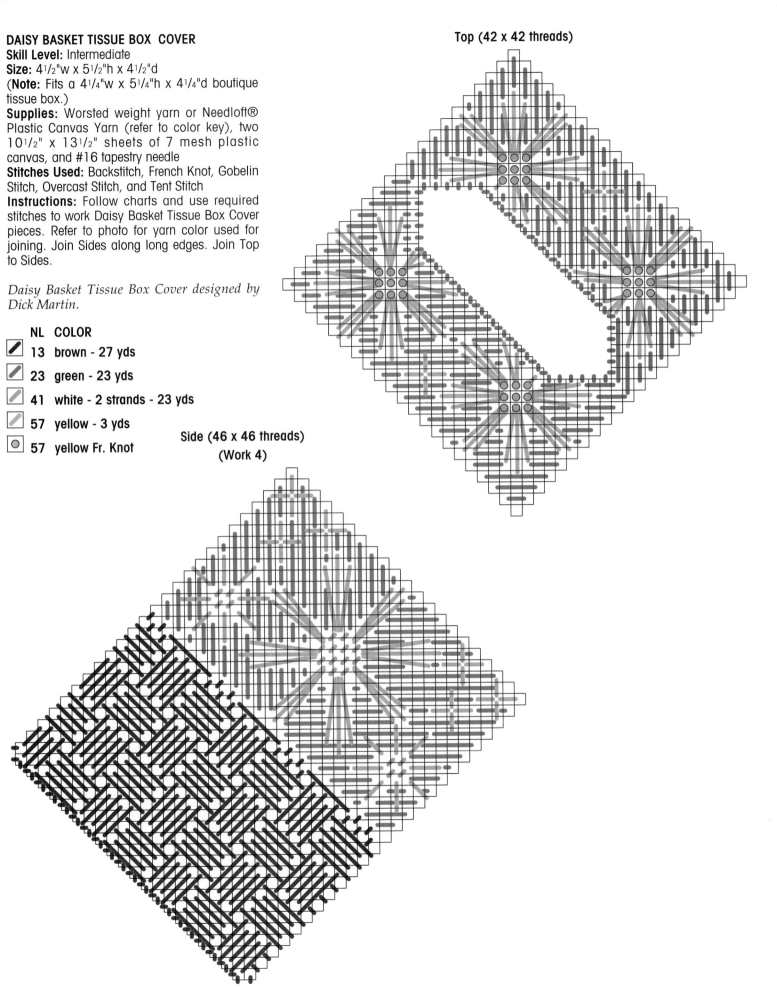

Top (42 x 42 threads)

Side (46 x 46 threads)
(Work 4)

A GIFT TO BANK ON

Invest in the future of your favorite young person with this "cent-sible" bank that's guaranteed to draw interest. Coins can be deposited through the slot in the roof and kept securely inside the little building. When a rainy day comes along, the money can be easily withdrawn through flaps on the bottom.

BANK

Skill Level: Intermediate

Size: 4"w x 4¼"h x 3¼"d

Supplies: Needloft® Plastic Canvas Yarn or worsted weight yarn (refer to color key), one 10½" x 13½" sheet of 7 mesh plastic canvas, and #16 tapestry needle

Stitches Used: Backstitch, Gobelin Stitch, Overcast Stitch, and Tent Stitch

Instructions: Follow charts and use required stitches to work Bank pieces. Use denim for all joining. Join Front and Back to Sides. Refer to photo to join Roof A to Roof B. Refer to photo to join Roof to Front, Back, and Sides. Match ★'s to join Bottom A to Front. Match ■'s to join Bottom B to Back. Join Bottom pieces to Sides through all thicknesses. To remove money, squeeze Bank to separate Bottom pieces.

Bank designed by Mary Billeaudeau.

NL	COLOR	
✎	01	red - 21 yds
✎	33	denim - 25 yds
✎	34	cerulean - 7 yds

Roof A (22 x 15 threads)

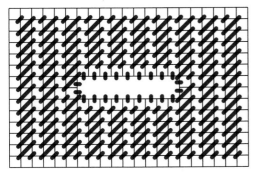

Roof B (22 x 15 threads)

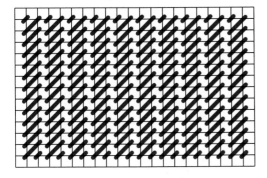

Side (22 x 22 threads) (Work 2)

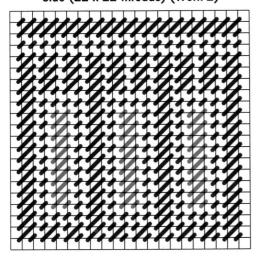

Bottom A (26 x 14 threads)

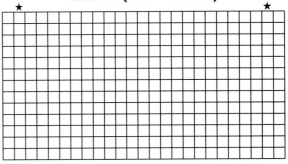

Bottom B (26 x 20 threads)

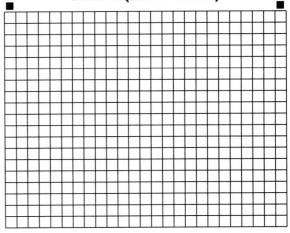

Front/Back (26 x 28 threads) (Work 2)

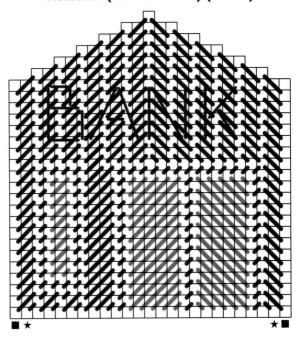

Soft and Pretty Sachets

Fragrant tokens of affection, sachets are thoughtful gifts anytime. This trio of floral sachets is stitched in soft, pretty colors that are sure to please a special lady.

FLORAL SACHETS
Skill Level: Beginner
Size: 3"w x 3" h
Supplies: Worsted weight yarn or Needloft® Plastic Canvas Yarn (refer to color key), one 10¹/₂" x 13¹/₂" sheet of 7 mesh plastic canvas, #16 tapestry needle, polyester fiberfill, and scented oil
Stitches Used: Gobelin Stitch, Overcast Stitch, and Tent Stitch

Instructions: Follow chart and use required stitches to work desired Floral Sachet. Refer to photo for yarn color used to join pieces. With wrong sides together, join pieces while lightly stuffing with scented fiberfill.

Floral Sachets designed by Ann Townsend.

NL	COLOR		NL	COLOR
05	dk pink		45	lt purple
07	pink		46	purple
35	blue		53	green
41	white			

Sachet #1 (21 x 21 threads) (Work 2)

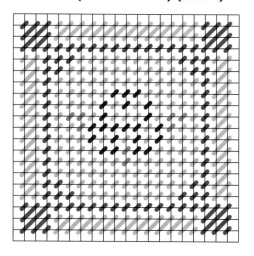

Sachet #2 (21 x 21 threads) (Work 2)

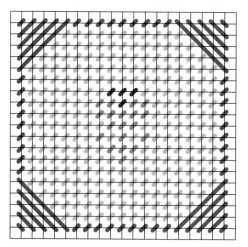

Sachet #3 (21 x 21 threads) (Work 2)

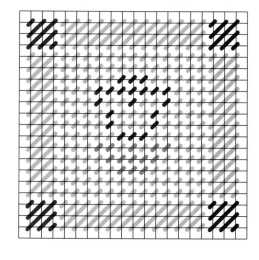

LADYBUG PLANT POKE

Skill Level: Beginner

Size: 3"w x 4³/₄"h

Supplies: Worsted weight yarn or Needloft® Plastic Canvas Yarn (refer to color key), one 10¹/₂" x 13¹/₂" sheet of 7 mesh plastic canvas, #16 tapestry needle, wooden skewer, 3" length of 3mm black chenille stem, and clear-drying craft glue

Stitches Used: Backstitch, Overcast Stitch, and Tent Stitch

Instructions: Follow chart and use required stitches to work Ladybug. Fold chenille stem in half. Refer to photo to bend and glue chenille stem to wrong side of Ladybug. Glue one end of wooden skewer to wrong side of Ladybug.

Ladybug Plant Poke designed by Dick Martin.

NL	COLOR
✎	00 black - 2 yds
✎	02 red - 4 yds

Ladybug (20 x 20 threads)

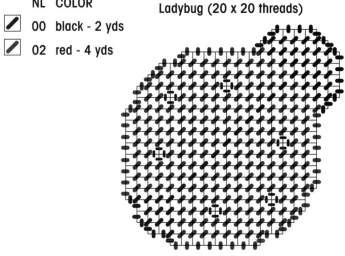

GUM BALL CLASSIC

Guaranteed to bring back sweet memories, this replica of an old-fashioned gum ball machine really works — the colorful treats are easily dispensed through an ingenious sliding compartment! Topped with a removable lid, the "glass" container is actually the recycled top of a plastic soft drink bottle. Metallic silver yarn trim adds a bit of authenticity to this classic piece of Americana.

GUM BALL MACHINE

Skill Level: Advanced

Size: 4³/₄"w x 10³/₄"h x 5¹/₄"d

Supplies: Needloft® Plastic Canvas Yarn or worsted weight yarn (refer to color keys), metallic silver yarn, one 12" x 18" sheet of clear 7 mesh plastic canvas, one 10¹/₂" x 13¹/₂" sheet of Christmas red 7 mesh plastic canvas, four 4¹/₂" dia plastic canvas circles, #16 tapestry needle, sewing needle, red sewing thread, one 2-liter plastic soda bottle, gum balls, and clear-drying craft glue

Stitches Used: Backstitch, Cross Stitch, Gobelin Stitch, Overcast Stitch, and Tent Stitch

Instructions: For Top, cut five threads from one plastic canvas circle. For Center Support, cut one thread from outer edge and two threads from center of one plastic canvas circle. For Bottom and Bottom Support, cut ten threads each from centers of two plastic canvas circles. Cut Top Rim, Center Rim, Base, Bottom Rim, Price Sign, Tray, Tray Rim, and Shaft Handles from clear plastic canvas. Cut remaining pieces from Christmas red plastic canvas. Follow charts and use required stitches to work Gum Ball Machine pieces, leaving stitches in shaded areas unworked. Unless otherwise indicated, use red for all joining. Match ▲'s and work stitches in shaded areas to join short ends of Top Rim, forming a cylinder. Refer to photo to join sections of Top Rim, forming a dome shape. Join Top to Top Rim. Use sewing thread and match ◆'s and ■'s to join one Sleeve Side to Sleeve Bottom. Use sewing thread and match ✚'s and ★'s to join remaining Sleeve Side to Sleeve Bottom. Use sewing thread and match ◆'s to join Chute Sides to Chute Slide. Use sewing thread and match ✿'s and ✖'s to join Chute to Sleeve Bottom. Use sewing thread and match ♠'s to join Sleeve Top to Sleeve Sides. Match ✿'s and ❖'s to join Sleeve to unworked threads on wrong side of Base. Join Sleeve to upper opening on wrong side of Base. Join Chute to lower opening on wrong side of Base. Join Base along short edges, forming a cylinder. Use sewing thread and match ▼'s to join Shaft Dividers to Shaft Tops. Use sewing thread to join Shaft Tops and Shaft Dividers to Shaft Sides along shaded threads. Use sewing thread and match ✱'s to join Shaft Back to Shaft Top and Shaft Sides. With wrong sides together, use metallic silver to join Shaft Handles, leaving area between ⊕'s unworked. Use metallic silver and match ⊛'s to join Shaft Handle to Shaft Front. Join Shaft Front to Shaft Top and Shaft Sides. Bending Shaft Back tabs, slide Shaft into Sleeve until tabs can extend from openings in Sleeve Sides. Use metallic silver and match ✢'s to join Tray Rim to Tray. Use metallic silver and match ◗'s to tack Tray and Tray Rim to Base. Join Center Rim along short edges, forming a cylinder. Join Center Rim to shaded thread of Center Support. Refer to photo and use metallic silver to join Center Support to Base. Use metallic silver to join Bottom Rim along short edges. Use metallic silver to join Bottom to Bottom Rim. Use metallic silver to join unworked edge of Bottom Rim to Bottom Support. Use metallic silver to join Bottom Support to Base. Cut 5¹/₂" away from bottom of clean bottle. Glue bottle opening to Center Support. Fill bottle with gum balls and place Top on bottle. Refer to photo to glue Price Sign to bottle.

Gum Ball Machine designed by Wayne Fox.

COLOR

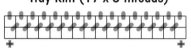 metallic silver

Tray Rim (17 x 3 threads)

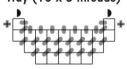

Chute Side (13 x 9 threads)
(Cut 2)

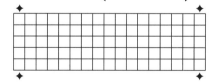

Sleeve Top (26 x 6 threads)

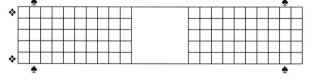

Tray (10 x 5 threads)

Chute Slide (18 x 6 threads)

Sleeve Side (26 x 6 threads) (Cut 2)

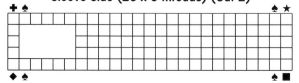

Sleeve Bottom (26 x 6 threads)

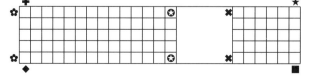

31

Bottom Support

Bottom

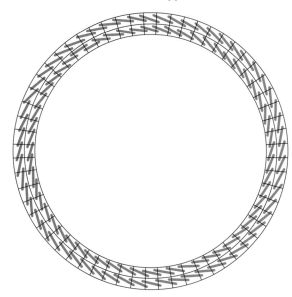

Shaft Side (24 x 5 threads) (Cut 2)

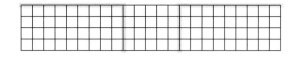

Price Sign
(10 x 11 threads)

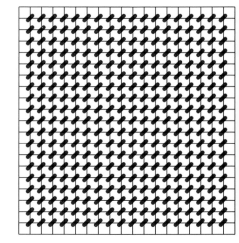

Shaft Top (10 x 5 threads)
(Cut 2)

Shaft Front
(5 x 5 threads)

Shaft Back
(9 x 5 threads)

Shaft Divider
(5 x 5 threads)
(Cut 2)

Shaft Handle
(6 x 6 threads)
(Work 2)

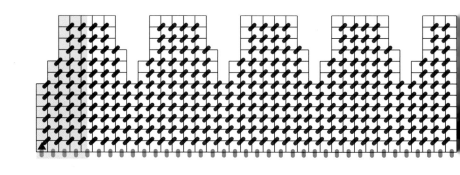

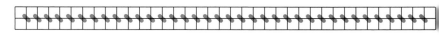

Center Support

Top

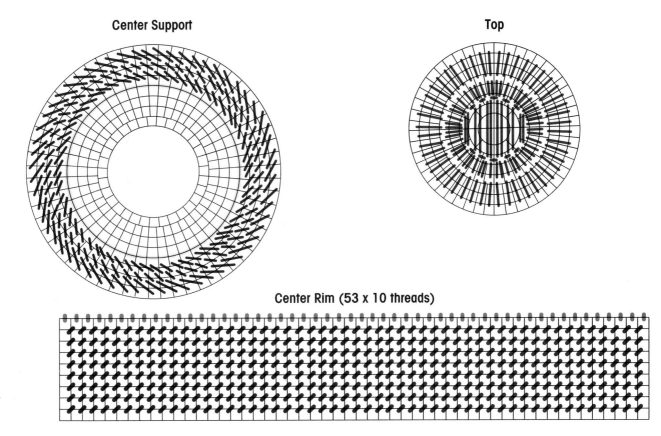

Center Rim (53 x 10 threads)

Base (83 x 21 threads)

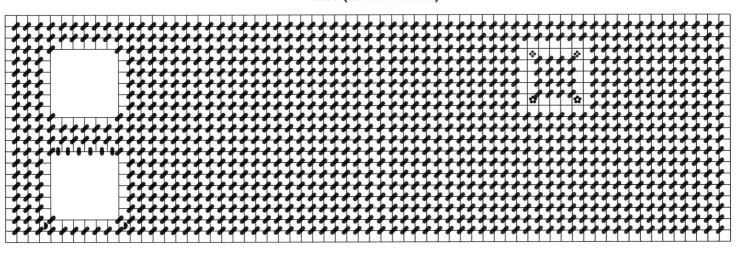

Top Rim (101 x 13 threads)

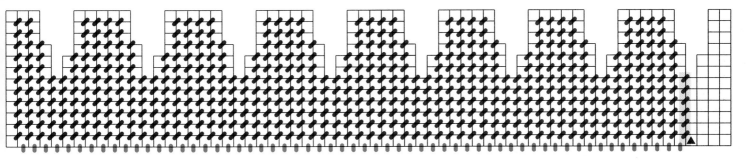

Bottom Rim (103 x 3 threads)

33

KEEP IN TOUCH

This attractive stationery organizer is a nice way to say "let's keep in touch" to a friend who's moving away. With compartments for everything from pens to envelopes, it can easily hold all the necessities for correspondence.

Wishing You Blessings

STATIONERY HOLDER

Skill Level: Advanced

Size: 6½"w x 9¾"h x 1⅛"d

Supplies: Worsted weight yarn or Needloft® Plastic Canvas Yarn (refer to color key), two 10½" x 13½" sheets of 7 mesh clear plastic canvas, two 10½" x 13½" sheets of 7 mesh white plastic canvas, #16 tapestry needle, two 10mm snaps, sewing needle, and white sewing thread

Stitches Used: Alternating Mosaic Stitch, Backstitch, Barred Square Stitch, Bound Cross Stitch, Cross Stitch, Gobelin Stitch, Long-legged Cross Stitch, Overcast Stitch, and Tent Stitch

Instructions: Cut Front, Back, Spine, Front Fasteners, and Back Fasteners from clear plastic canvas. Cut remaining pieces from white plastic canvas. Follow charts and use required stitches to work Stationery Holder pieces. Use sewing needle and thread to join snaps to wrong sides of Front Fasteners and right sides of Back Fasteners. Use white for all joining. Match ▲'s to join unworked edges of Stamp Holder to Inner Pocket B. Join Envelope Holder Short Sides to Envelope Holder Long Side along short edges. Join Envelope Holder Sides to Envelope Holder Front along unworked edges. Match ★'s to join Envelope Holder Sides to Inner Pocket B. Join Pen Holder Long Sides to Pen Holder Short Side along short edges. Join Pen Holder Sides to Pen Holder Front along unworked edges. Match ✪'s to join Pen Holder Sides to Inner Pocket B. Refer to Diagram to place Inner Pocket B on wrong side of Back.

(**Note:** Shaded areas on Diagram indicate wrong sides of stitched pieces.) Match ✱'s for placement of Back Fasteners. Join Inner Pocket B and Back Fasteners to Back, leaving long inner edge of Inner Pocket B open. Refer to Diagram to place Inner Pocket A on wrong side of Front. Match ■'s for placement of Front Fasteners. Refer to Diagram for placement of Spine. Join Inner Pocket A, Front Fasteners, and Spine to Front, leaving short upper edge of Inner Pocket A open. Join Back to Spine. Use white Overcast Stitches to cover unworked edges of Front, Back, and Spine.

Stationery Holder designed by Linda Smith.

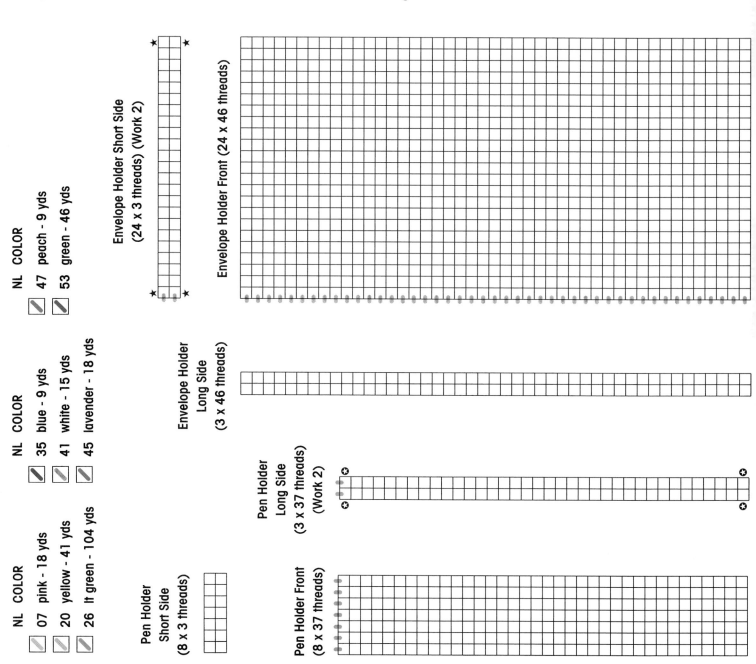

NL	COLOR
07	pink - 18 yds
20	yellow - 41 yds
26	lt green - 104 yds
35	blue - 9 yds
41	white - 15 yds
45	lavender - 18 yds
47	peach - 9 yds
53	green - 46 yds

Envelope Holder Short Side (24 x 3 threads) (Work 2)

Envelope Holder Front (24 x 46 threads)

Envelope Holder Long Side (3 x 46 threads)

Pen Holder Long Side (3 x 37 threads) (Work 2)

Pen Holder Short Side (8 x 3 threads)

Pen Holder Front (8 x 37 threads)

Spine (7 x 65 threads)

Front/Back (43 x 65 threads) (Work 2)

Diagram

Front
F
F
Inner Pocket A
Spine
Back
Envelope Holder
Stamp Holder
Inner Pocket B
Pen Holder
F
F

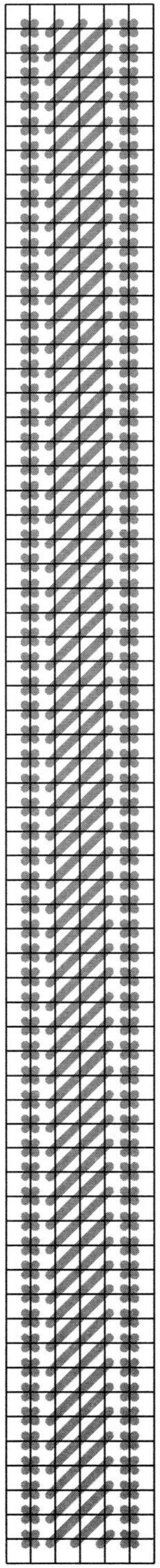

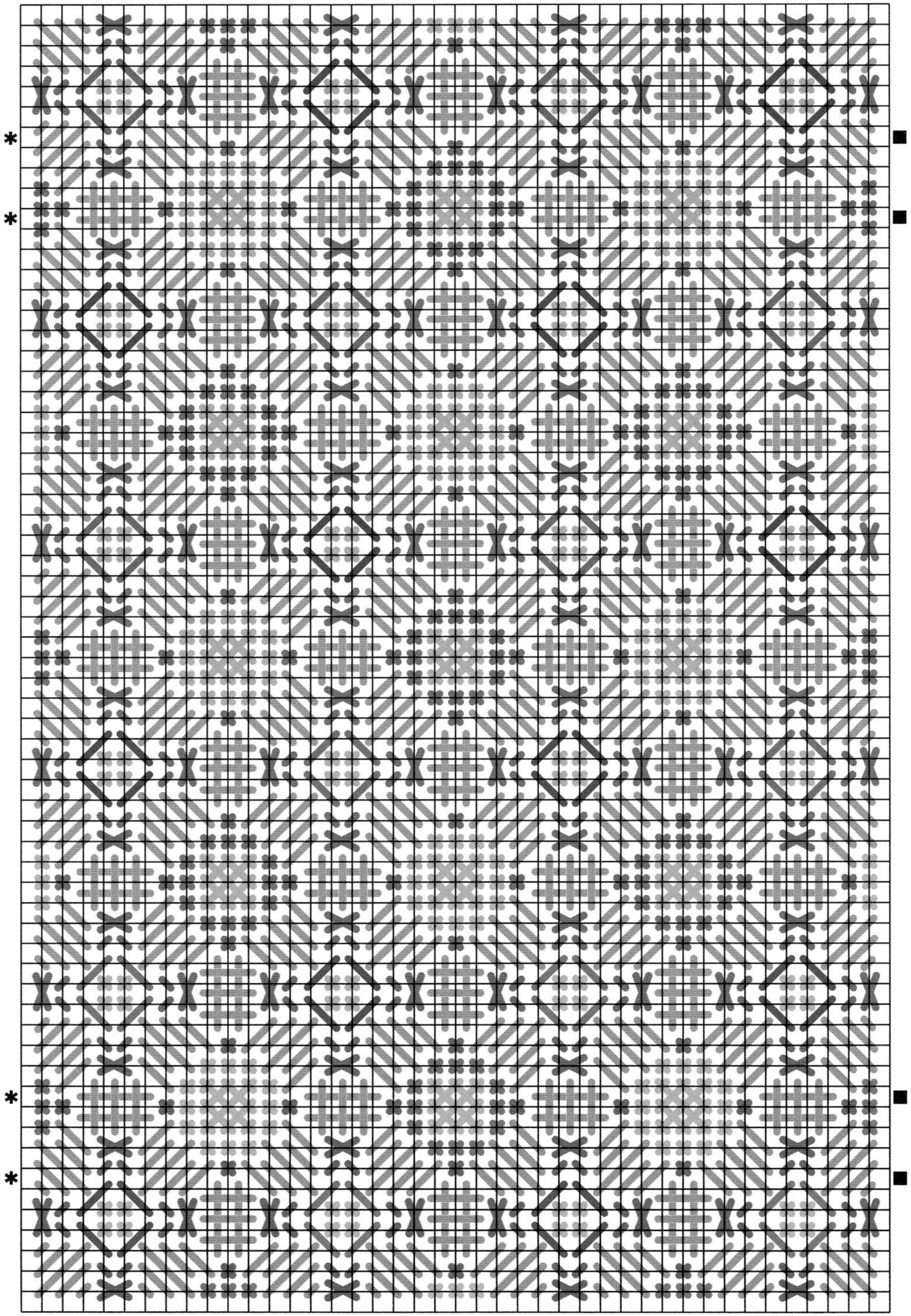

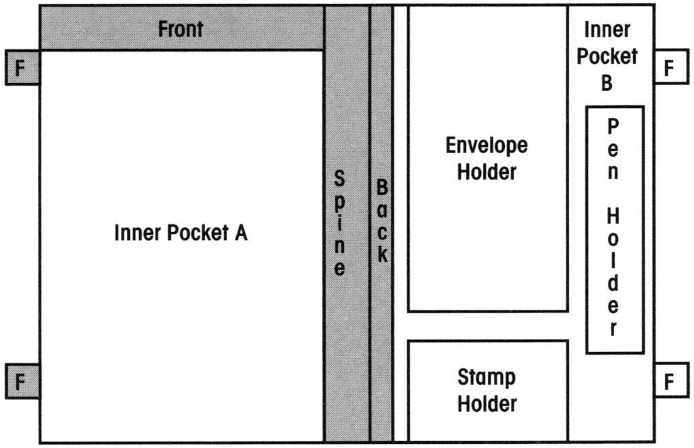

Front Fastener
(6 x 6 threads)
(Work 2)

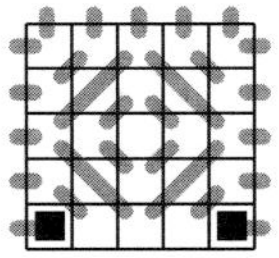

Back Fastener
(6 x 6 threads)
(Work 2)

Stamp Holder (24 x 16 threads)

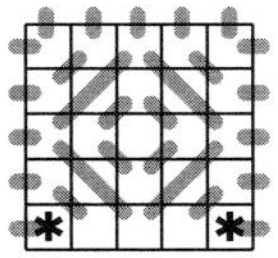

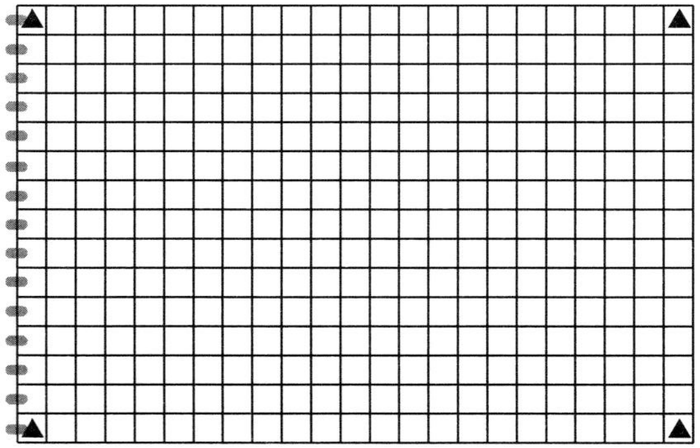

Inner Pocket B (40 x 65 threads)

Inner Pocket A (43 x 59 threads)

A TO Z BOOKENDS

Encourage a youngster's love for reading with a set of these brightly colored bookend covers! Presented with several children's books, the clever projects are sure to stimulate a child's interest in learning about everything from apples to zebras!

A TO Z BOOKEND COVERS

Skill Level: Intermediate
Size: 5"w x 5½"h x 2"d
(**Note:** Fit 4¾"w x 5"h bookends.)
Supplies: Worsted weight yarn or Needloft® Plastic Canvas Yarn (refer to color key), two 10½" x 13½" sheets of 7 mesh clear plastic canvas, #16 tapestry needle, two purchased bookends, and clear-drying craft glue
Stitches Used: Backstitch, French Knot, Gobelin Stitch, Overcast Stitch, and Tent Stitch
Instructions: Follow charts and use required stitches to work Bookend pieces, leaving stitches in shaded area unworked. Use green and match ★'s to join A Bookend Front to A Base. Refer to photo and use red to tack Apple to A Bookend Front and A Base. Use yarn color to match stitching area to join Back to wrong side of A Bookend Front. Use green and match ✘'s to join Z Bookend Front to Z Base. With right sides facing up, match ▲'s and work stitches in shaded area through two thicknesses to join Zebra to Zebra Support. Use blue and match ■'s to tack Zebra Support to Z Bookend Front. Use black to tack Zebra to Z Base. Use color to match stitching area to join Back to wrong side of Z Bookend Front. For tail, cut three 12" lengths and two 8" lengths of black yarn. Fold three 12" yarn lengths in half and secure fold with one 8" yarn length. Braid for 2" and secure end of braid with remaining yarn length. Trim ends to ½". Remove yarn securing fold. Glue folded end of tail to wrong side of Zebra.

Bookend Covers designed by Dick Martin.

NL	COLOR		NL	COLOR
00	black - 5 yds		41	white - 4 yds
02	red - 4 yds		57	yellow - 9 yds
23	green - 12 yds		00	black Fr. Knot
32	blue - 20 yds		57	yellow Fr. Knot

A Bookend Front/Back (34 x 37 threads) (Cut 2, Work 1)

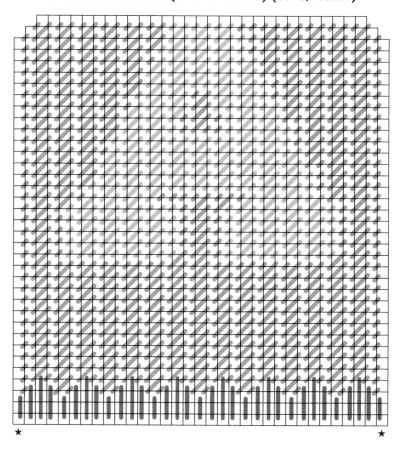

Apple (28 x 24 threads)

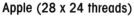
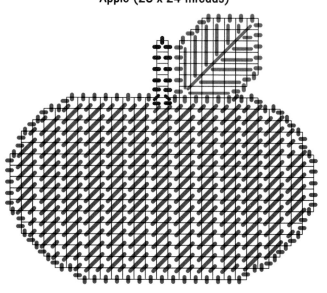

A Base (34 x 14 threads)

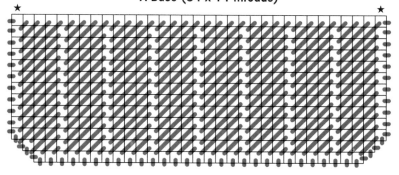

Z Bookend Front/Back (34 x 37 threads) (Cut 2, Work 1)

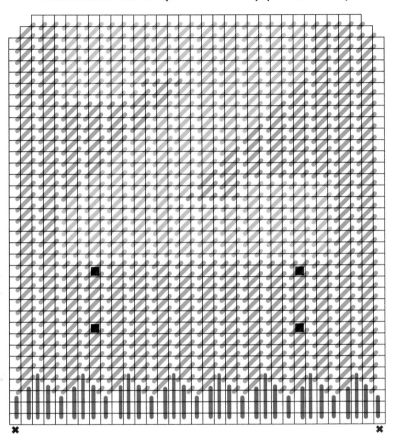

Zebra (27 x 25 threads)

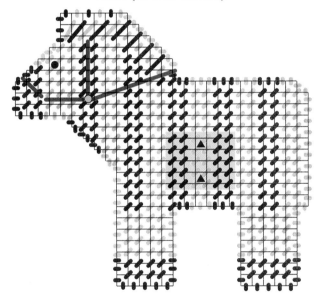

Z Base (34 x 14 threads)

Zebra Support (24 x 7 threads)

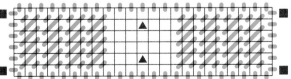

POTPOURRI TEACUP

Filled with fragrant petals, this pretty teacup potpourri holder is a sweet-smelling way to let a friend know she's in your thoughts. A dainty floral border encircles the cup, making it a charming accent for the bedroom or bath. The sentimental gift is certain to be a pleasant reminder of your friendship.

TEACUP POTPOURRI HOLDER

Skill Level: Intermediate

Size: 2½"h x 4½" dia

Supplies: Worsted weight yarn or Needloft® Plastic Canvas Yarn (refer to color key), one 10½" x 13½" sheet of 7 mesh plastic canvas, two 4" dia plastic canvas circles, one 9" dia plastic canvas circle, and #16 tapestry needle

Stitches Used: Cross Stitch, Gobelin Stitch, Overcast Stitch, and Tent Stitch

Instructions: For Saucer Rim, cut a piece of plastic canvas 90 x 3 threads. For Teacup Lower Side, trim sixteen threads from outer edge of 9" dia plastic canvas circle. Trim seven threads from center. Refer to chart to trim away excess canvas. For Teacup Bottom, trim ten threads from 4" dia plastic canvas circle. Follow charts and use required stitches to work Teacup Potpourri Holder pieces. Use white for all joining. Join Teacup Upper Side along short edges. Match ▲'s to join short edges of Teacup Lower Side. Join Teacup Bottom to Teacup Lower Side. Refer to photo to join Teacup Upper Side to Teacup Lower Side. With wrong sides together join Handle Side A to Handle Side B. Refer to photo to join Handle to Teacup Upper Side and Teacup Lower Side. Join Saucer Rim along short edges. Join Saucer Rim to Saucer. Refer to photo to tack Teacup to Saucer.

Teacup Potpourri Holder designed by Kooler Design Studio.

NL	COLOR
07	pink - 2 yds
35	blue - 5 yds
39	ecru - 4 yds
41	white - 20 yds
53	green - 2 yds

Handle Side A
(9 x 12 threads)

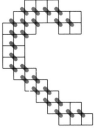

Handle Side B
(9 x 12 threads)

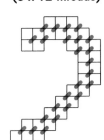

Saucer

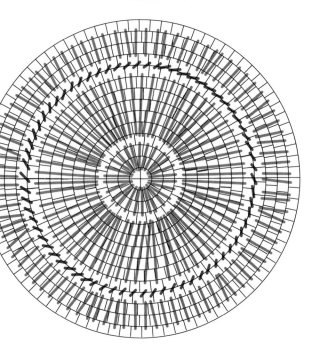

Teacup Lower Side

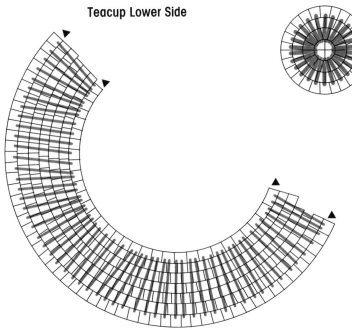

Teacup Bottom

Teacup Upper Side (55 x 8 threads)

Saucer Rim (90 x 3 threads)

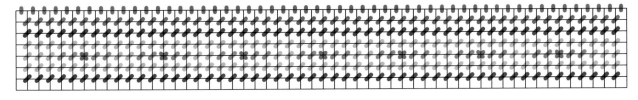

"GET WELL" WISHES

Let this cheery floral sign deliver "get well" wishes to a friend who's home sick or in the hospital. Designed to hang from the knob on a door or a chest of drawers, its perky colors are sure to brighten the day!

"GET WELL SOON" DOOR SIGN

Skill Level: Beginner

Size: 5"w x 11⅞"h

Supplies: Worsted weight yarn or Needloft® Plastic Canvas Yarn (refer to color key), one 10½" x 13½" sheet of 7 mesh plastic canvas, and #16 tapestry needle

Stitches Used: Backstitch, Gobelin Stitch, Mosaic Stitch, Overcast Stitch, and Tent Stitch

Instructions: Follow charts and use required stitches to work "Get Well Soon" Door Sign pieces. Refer to photo to tack Flower to Door Sign.

"Get Well Soon" Door Sign designed by Dick Martin.

NL	COLOR
07	pink - 10 yds
12	orange - 2 yds
20	yellow - 2 yds
26	lt green - 4 yds
53	green - 10 yds

Flower (12 x 12 threads)

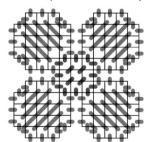

Door Sign (34 x 79 threads)

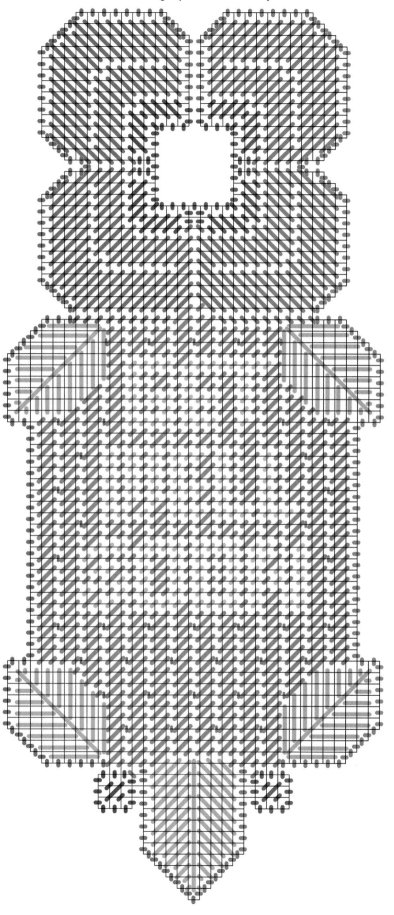

FLOWER GARDEN MAGNETS

Capture the beauty of a flower garden with these lovely magnets. The dainty stick-ups make sweet "thinking of you" gifts for any reason — or no reason at all. Why not make lots of them for sharing a breath of spring all through the year!

FLORAL MAGNETS

Skill Level: Intermediate
Approx Size: 3½"w x 3"h x ½"d
Supplies: Worsted weight yarn or Needloft® Plastic Canvas Yarn (refer to color key), one 10½" x 13½" sheet of 7 mesh plastic canvas, #16 tapestry needle, 8" lengths of ¹/₁₆"w or ¼"w satin ribbon (refer to photo), magnetic strip, and clear-drying craft glue
Stitches Used: Backstitch, Cross Stitch, French Knot, Gobelin Stitch, Overcast Stitch, and Tent Stitch
Instructions: Follow charts and use required stitches to work desired Magnet pieces, leaving stitches in shaded area unworked. Refer to photo to glue Flowers and Leaves to Wreath, Vase, Basket, and Bouquet. Refer to photo to tie ribbons in a bow and trim ends. Glue bow to Magnet. Trim magnetic strip to desired size and glue to wrong side of stitched piece.
For Pot only: Refer to photo to place Petals on Pot Back. Work stitches in shaded area through three thicknesses to join Petals to Pot Back. Place Pot Back on unworked Pot Back. Use yarn color to match stitching area to join Pot Back pieces above ▲'s and between ★'s. With right sides facing up, use blue to join Pot Front to Pot Back pieces.

Basket and Pot designed by Dick Martin.
Wreath designed by Eileen Dobbratz.

NL	COLOR
07	lt pink
13	lt brown
26	lt green
35	blue
41	white
53	green
57	yellow
	Flower #1 color
	Flower #2 color
07	lt pink Fr. Knot
20	lt yellow Fr. Knot

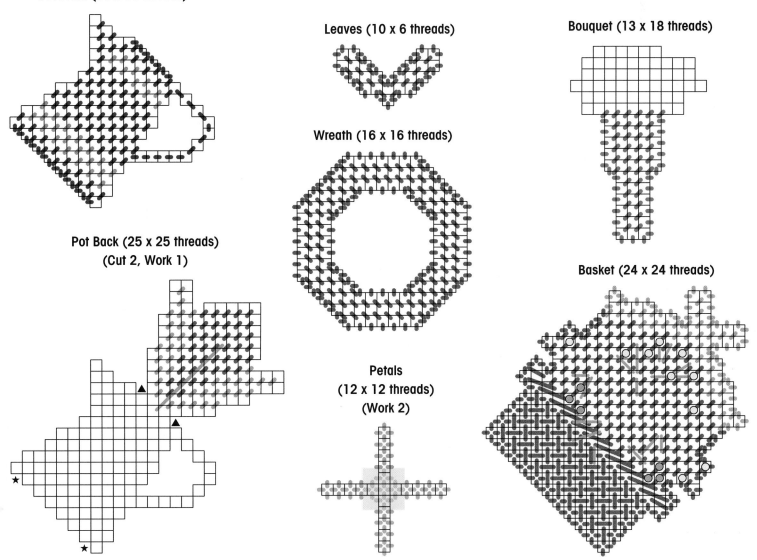

Flower #1 (4 x 4 threads)

Flower #2 (6 x 6 threads)

Vase (11 x 20 threads)

Pot Front (19 x 18 threads)

Leaves (10 x 6 threads)

Bouquet (13 x 18 threads)

Wreath (16 x 16 threads)

Pot Back (25 x 25 threads) (Cut 2, Work 1)

Petals (12 x 12 threads) (Work 2)

Basket (24 x 24 threads)

47

A Sure-Cure Gift

This decorative tissue box cover is a wonderful way to help cheer up a friend who's got the sniffles. Its pretty pattern uses a combination of Gobelin and Alicia Lace stitches, and the colors can be changed to match any decor. For an especially thoughtful gift, present it with a box of soft tissues inside and include a bouquet of flowers.

DECORATIVE TISSUE BOX COVER

Skill Level: Beginner

Size: 4³/₄"w x 5³/₄"h x 4³/₄"d

(**Note:** Fits a 4¹/₄"w x 5¹/₄"h x 4¹/₄"d boutique tissue box.)

Supplies: Worsted weight yarn or Needloft® Plastic Canvas Yarn (refer to color key), one 10¹/₂" x 13¹/₂" sheet of 7 mesh plastic canvas, and #16 tapestry needle

Stitches Used: Alicia Lace, Gobelin Stitch, Overcast Stitch, and Tent Stitch

Instructions: Follow charts and use required stitches to work Tissue Box Cover pieces. Use dk pink to join pieces. Join Sides along long edges. Join Top to Sides.

Decorative Tissue Box Cover designed by Wera Harrison.

NL	COLOR
▱	05 dk pink - 24 yds
▱	07 pink - 40 yds

Top (30 x 30 threads)

Side (30 x 38 threads) (Work 4)

BE-HAPPY BEE

A cheery pick-me-up for a friend who's feeling down, this bright-eyed bee is all abuzz about spreading sunshine. The cute stick-up is easily attached with suction cups to windows or any glass surface. Wearing a broad smile and a snazzy bow tie, our little friend shares the sentiment, "Don't worry, 'Bee' Happy!"

BEE HAPPY STICK-UP

Skill Level: Intermediate

Size: 5⅝"w x 6½"h

Supplies: Worsted weight yarn or Needloft® Plastic Canvas Yarn (refer to color key), one 10½" x 13½" sheet of 7 mesh plastic canvas, #16 tapestry needle, 8" length of 3mm black chenille stem, two 20mm suction cups, two 15mm moving eyes, and clear-drying craft glue

Stitches Used: Backstitch, French Knot, Gobelin Stitch, Overcast Stitch, Tent Stitch, and Triple Cross Stitch

Instructions: Follow charts and use required stitches to work Stick-up pieces. Insert and glue suction cups into openings in Front at ▲'s. Cut chenille stem in half. Refer to photo to bend and glue chenille stem pieces to wrong side of Front. With wrong sides together, use color to match stitching area to join Front to Back along unworked edges. Refer to photo to glue Nose, Bow Tie, and moving eyes to Front. For mouth, cut a 3" length of black yarn. Refer to photo to shape and glue black yarn to Front.

Bee Happy Stick-up designed by Sandy and Honey for Studio M.

NL	COLOR
00	black - 23 yds
22	green - 1 yd
56	yellow - 15 yds
58	orange - 3 yds
58	orange Fr. Knot

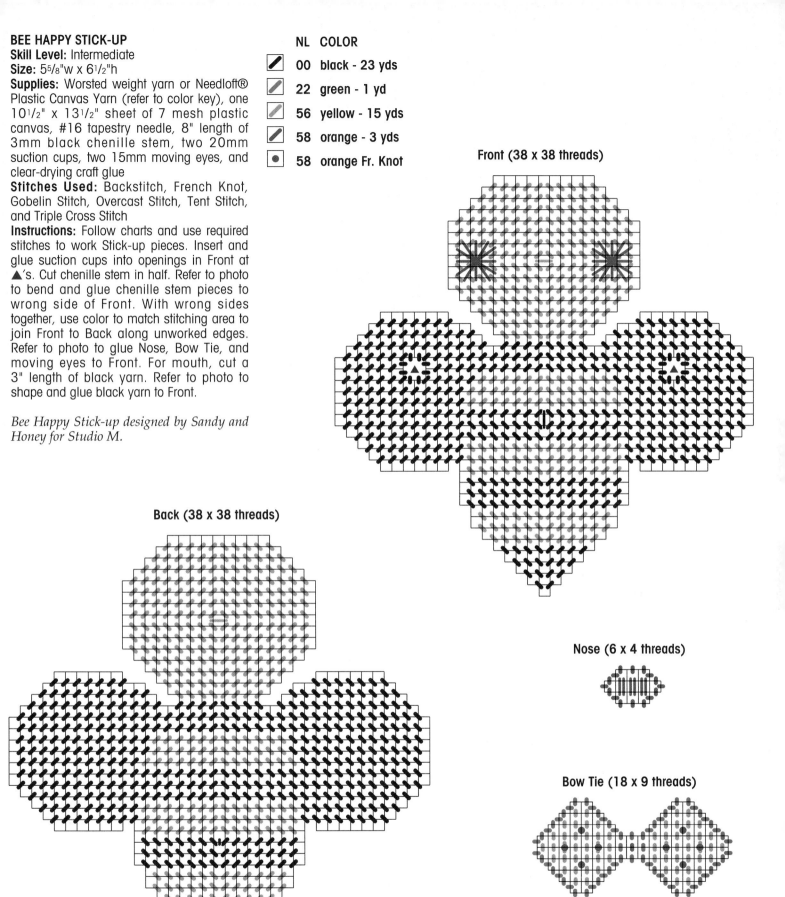

Front (38 x 38 threads)

Back (38 x 38 threads)

Nose (6 x 4 threads)

Bow Tie (18 x 9 threads)

"Beary" Special Relatives

Show family members that they're appreciated with these adorable personalized magnets! Perfect as thank-you gifts, forget-me-nots, or for any family occasion, they're "beary" special reminders of your love. The miniature flocked bears can be positioned anywhere along the rainbow to punctuate your sweet sentiments.

SPECIAL RELATIVES MAGNET

Skill Level: Beginner

Size: 4¹/₈"w x 2⁵/₈"h x ³/₄"d

Supplies: Worsted weight yarn or Needloft® Plastic Canvas Yarn (refer to color key), six-strand black embroidery floss, one 10¹/₂" x 13¹/₂" sheet of 7 mesh plastic canvas, #16 tapestry needle, 1" flocked bear, magnetic strip, and clear-drying craft glue

Stitches Used: Backstitch, Overcast Stitch, and Tent Stitch

Instructions: Follow chart and use required stitches to work Magnet. Refer to photo to center and stitch desired name. Refer to photo to glue flocked bear to Magnet. Trim magnetic strip to desired size and glue to wrong side of stitched piece.

Special Relatives Magnets designed by Toni Erwin.

NL	COLOR
01	red - 1 yd
28	green - 1 yd
32	blue - 2 yds
41	white - 4 yds
57	yellow - 1 yd
58	orange -1 yd
	black embroidery floss - 2 yds

Magnet (28 x 18 threads)

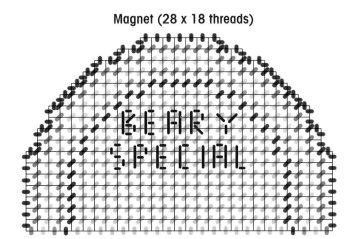

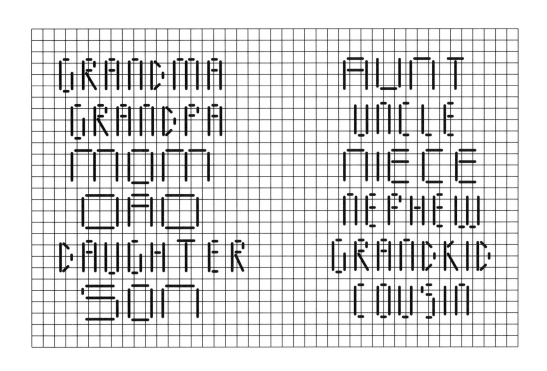

For Your Favorite Folks

These fun magnets are great for saying "you're special" to a friend or family member. The cute messages will put a smile on anyone's face!

MAGNETS
Skill Level: Beginner
Approx Size: 4"w x 4"h each
Supplies: Worsted weight yarn or Needloft® Plastic Canvas Yarn (refer to color key), 6-strand embroidery floss (refer to color key), one 10½" x 13½" sheet of 7 mesh plastic canvas, #16 tapestry needle, magnetic strip, and clear-drying craft glue
Stitches Used: Backstitch, Overcast Stitch, and Tent Stitch
Instructions: Follow chart and use required stitches to work Magnet. Trim magnetic strip to desired size and glue to wrong side of stitched piece.

Magnets designed by Kathleen Hurley.

NL	COLOR
01	red - 6 yds
15	brown - 2 yds
28	green - 1 yd
29	dk green - 1 yd
39	ecru - 6 yds
43	tan - 2 yds
	blue embroidery floss - 2 yds
	black embroidery floss - 2 yds

Apple (21 x 26 threads)

Cup (34 x 22 threads)

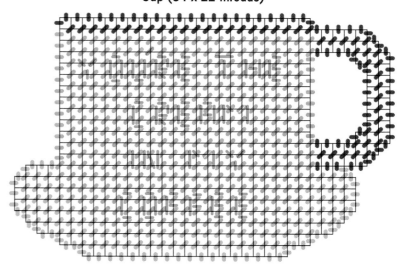

54

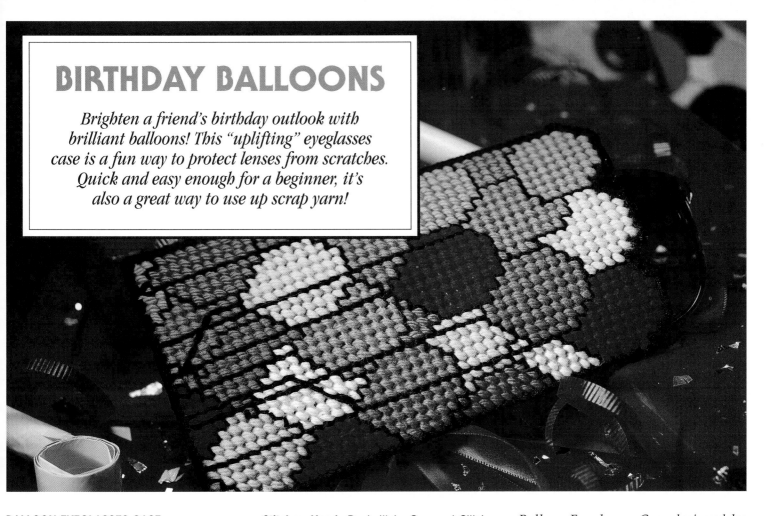

BIRTHDAY BALLOONS

Brighten a friend's birthday outlook with brilliant balloons! This "uplifting" eyeglasses case is a fun way to protect lenses from scratches. Quick and easy enough for a beginner, it's also a great way to use up scrap yarn!

BALLOON EYEGLASSES CASE
Skill Level: Beginner
Size: 3³/₄"w x 6³/₄"h
Supplies: Worsted weight yarn or Needloft® Plastic Canvas Yarn (refer to color key), one 10¹/₂" x 13¹/₂" sheet of 7 mesh plastic canvas, and #16 tapestry needle

Stitches Used: Backstitch, Overcast Stitch, and Tent Stitch
Instructions: Follow chart and use required stitches to work Balloon Eyeglasses Case pieces. With wrong sides together, use black to join Front to Back along unworked edges.

Balloon Eyeglasses Case designed by Kathy Sarnelli.

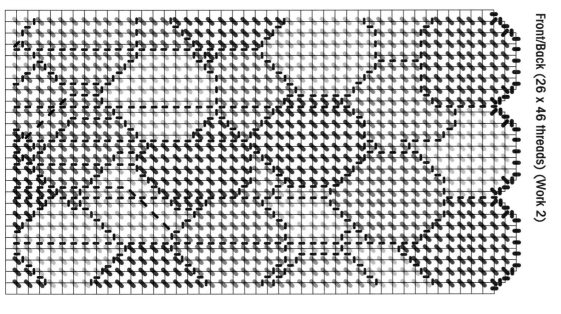

Front/Back (26 x 46 threads) (Work 2)

NL	COLOR		NL	COLOR
00	black - 15 yds		51	lt green - 3 yds
02	red - 7 yds		55	melon - 4 yds
28	green - 5 yds		57	yellow - 6 yds
35	blue - 5 yds		59	purple - 6 yds
44	pink - 3 yds			

A CUP OF FRIENDSHIP

This charming teacup magnet is a sweet token of friendship, and it's so easy you can probably finish it before the kettle whistles! The double-sided magnet is left open at the top to form a pocket for holding a tea bag. A heart-shaped gift tag, tied onto the bag's string, can be penned with poetry, an encouraging thought, or any sentiment appropriate for the occasion.

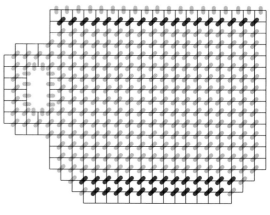

A LITTLE CUP OF FRIENDSHIP, WITH A BAG OF TEA. WHEN YOU DRINK THIS THINK OF LOVE FROM ME!

CUP OF TEA MAGNET

Skill Level: Beginner

Size: 3 1/2"w x 2 3/4"h

Supplies: Needloft® Plastic Canvas Yarn or worsted weight yarn (refer to color key), one 10 1/2" x 13 1/2" sheet of 7 mesh plastic canvas, #16 tapestry needle, magnetic strip, and clear-drying craft glue

Stitches Used: Overcast Stitch and Tent Stitch

Instructions: Follow charts and use required stitches to work Magnet pieces.

With wrong sides together, use eggshell to join Front to Back along unworked edges. Glue magnetic strip to Back.

Cup of Tea Magnet designed by Fran Way Bohler.

NL COLOR

 33 denim - 3 yds

 39 eggshell - 9 yds

Front (24 x 18 threads)

Back (24 x 18 threads)

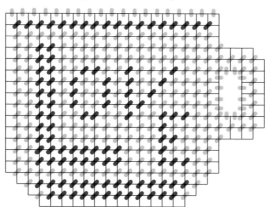

CHECKMATE COASTERS

Show a special fellow that he's your knight in shining armor with this handsome chess coaster set. It's perfect for the den or the office! Each game piece is regally represented on a coaster that will "checkmate" water rings, and they can all be conveniently stored in the distinctive matching box.

CHESS COASTER SET

Skill Level: Beginner
Coaster Size: 4¹/₂"w x 4¹/₂"h each
Coaster Box Size: 4³/₄"w x 2"h x 4³/₄"d
Supplies: Needloft® Plastic Canvas yarn or worsted weight yarn (refer to color key), two 10¹/₂" x 13¹/₂" sheets of 7 mesh plastic canvas, #16 tapestry needle, cork or felt, and clear-drying craft glue
Stitches Used: Alternating Scotch Stitch, Backstitch, Gobelin Stitch, Overcast Stitch, and Tent Stitch

Instructions: Follow charts and use required stitches to work Chess Coaster Set pieces. Cut cork or felt slightly smaller than Coasters and glue to wrong side of stitched pieces. Use gold to join Top Sides along short edges. Use gold to join Top to Top Sides. For Bottom, cut a piece of plastic canvas 32 x 32 threads. (**Note:** Bottom is not worked.) Use black to join Bottom Sides along short edges. Use black to join Bottom to Bottom Sides.

Chess Coaster Set designed by Diane W. Villano.

NL	COLOR
✎	00 black - 73 yds
✎	02 Christmas red - 57 yds
✎	17 gold - 23 yds
✎	41 white - 29 yds

Bottom Side (32 x 13 threads) (Work 4)

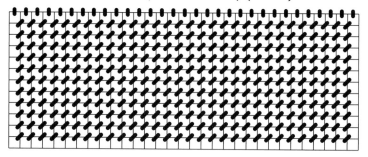

Top Side (34 x 6 threads) (Work 4)

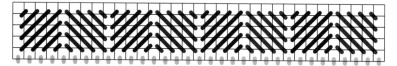

Top (34 x 34 threads)

King Coaster (30 x 30 threads)

Queen Coaster (30 x 30 threads)

Bishop Coaster (30 x 30 threads)

Rook Coaster (30 x 30 threads)

Knight Coaster (30 x 30 threads)

Pawn Coaster (30 x 30 threads)

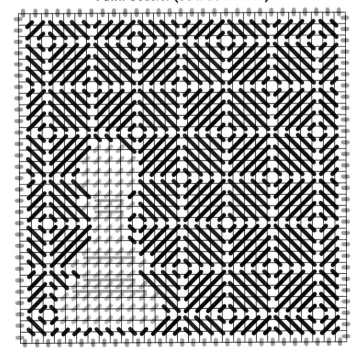

FLORAL BOOKMARK

Skill Level: Beginner
Size: 2¹/₈"w x 7¹/₂"h
Supplies: DMC #3 pearl cotton or 12 strands of embroidery floss (refer to color key), one 10¹/₂" x 13¹/₂" sheet each of light blue, wedgewood green, ivory, yellow, and beige 10 mesh plastic canvas, and #20 tapestry needle
Stitches Used: Backstitch, Gobelin Stitch, and Tent Stitch
Instructions: Cut Base from ivory plastic canvas. Cut Large Flowers and Buds from light blue plastic canvas. Cut Centers from beige plastic canvas. Cut Small Flowers from yellow plastic canvas. Cut Leaves from wedgewood green plastic canvas. Follow chart and use required stitches to work Base. Match ✿'s to place Large Flowers on Base. Work stitches on Large Flowers to join Large Flowers to Base. Match ✱'s to place Centers on Large Flowers. Work stitches on Centers to join Centers to Large Flowers and Base. Refer to photo and match like symbols to place Leaves, Buds, and Small Flowers on Base. Work stitches on Leaves, Buds, and Small Flowers to join pieces to Base.

Floral Bookmark designed by Dick Martin.

⧄ **469 green**	⧄ **726 yellow**
⧄ **471 lt green**	⧄ **828 blue**
⧄ **676 gold**	

HEARTS AND FLOWERS BOOKMARK

A friend who loves to read will treasure this novel gift idea! Our floral bookmark is stitched with pearl cotton on colored 10 mesh canvas. To make your offering especially nice, tuck the marker inside a favorite book.

Large Flower
(10 x 10 threads)
(Cut 3)

Leaf
(6 x 6 threads)
(Cut 2)

Bud
(4 x 4 threads)
(Cut 4)

Small Flower
(4 x 4 threads)
(Cut 2)

Center
(4 x 4 threads)
(Cut 3)

Base (60 x 60 threads)

ELEGANT WEDDING ALBUM

This romantic album cover offers a uniquely personal gift for the lucky couple. Designed to frame a wedding photograph or invitation, the front is trimmed with golden cord and bells. What a lovely way to display keepsakes of their special day!

WEDDING ALBUM COVER

Skill Level: Intermediate

Size: 10¼"w x 12"h x 2⅝"d

(**Note:** Fits a 9½"w x 11½"h x 2½"d photo album and holds a 5"w x 7"h photograph.)

Supplies: White worsted weight yarn or Needloft® Plastic Canvas Yarn, metallic gold cord, three 10½" x 13½" sheets of 7 mesh plastic canvas, #16 tapestry needle, photo album, and clear-drying craft glue

Stitches Used: Alternating Scotch Stitch, Backstitch, Gobelin Stitch, Overcast Stitch, and Tent Stitch

Instructions: Follow charts and use required stitches to work Wedding Album Cover pieces, leaving stitches in shaded areas unworked. For Back, cut a piece of plastic canvas 68 x 80 threads. Use white Alternating Scotch Stitches over three threads to work Back. For Photo Backing, cut a piece of plastic canvas 38 x 50 threads. Match Photo Backing edges to shaded areas on wrong side of Front. Work stitches in shaded areas to join Photo Backing to Front. Use white for all joining. Refer to photo to join Spine to Front and Back along long edges. For Sleeves, cut two pieces of plastic canvas 15 x 80 threads each. Match corners of Sleeve to ▲'s on wrong side of Front to join Sleeve to Front. Repeat for Back and remaining Sleeve. Use white Overcast Stitches to cover unworked edges of Front, Back, and Spine. For bow, cut an 8" length of metallic gold cord. Tie cord in a bow and trim ends. Refer to photo to glue Bells and bow to Front.

Wedding Album Cover designed by Dick Martin.

NL COLOR

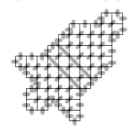

41 white - 187 yds

metallic gold cord - 19 yds

Bell (11 x 11 threads) (Work 2)

Spine (18 x 80 threads)

Front (68 x 80 threads)

This cute chatelaine makes a sweet friendship gift for a "beary" special seamstress. Quick to stitch, the lovable little bear and a pair of scissors are attached to opposite ends of a length of ribbon and worn around the neck. What a clever way to keep a sewing essential handy!

CHATELAINE

Skill Level: Beginner

Bear Size: 2⁵/₈"w x 4"h

Supplies: Worsted weight yarn or Needloft® Plastic Canvas Yarn (refer to color key), one 10¹/₂" x 13¹/₂" sheet of 7 mesh plastic canvas, #16 tapestry needle, 48" of ³/₈"w blue grosgrain ribbon, scissors, sewing needle, and thread

Stitches Used: Backstitch, Cross Stitch, French Knot, Overcast Stitch, and Tent Stitch

Instructions: Follow chart and use required stitches to work Bear. Refer to photo to thread ends of ribbon through Bear and scissors. Fold ribbon ends under and sew in place.

Chatelaine designed by Kathie Rueger.

NL	COLOR
	black 2-ply
01	red
13	brown
15	dk brown
	dk brown 2-ply
40	tan
00	black Fr. Knot

Bear (18 x 27 threads)

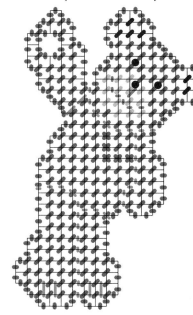

FISHING FOR FUN

This whimsical fishing pond is a fun way to help a preschooler catch on to learning numbers and colors. The rod has a magnet glued to the end of the line that "hooks" paper clips extending from the fishes' mouths. As each fish is caught, the child can identify its color and the number on its side.

FISHING SET

Skill Level: Intermediate
Pond Size: 9¼"w x 9¼"h x 10"d
Supplies: Needloft® Plastic Canvas Yarn or worsted weight yarn (refer to color key), three 10½" x 13½" sheets of clear 7 mesh plastic canvas, one 10½" x 13½" sheet of dark blue 7 mesh plastic canvas, #16 tapestry needle, two ¾" dia magnets, two 13" lengths of coat hanger wire, ten jumbo wire paper clips, twenty 6mm moving eyes, hot glue gun, and glue sticks
Stitches Used: Backstitch, Cross Stitch, Gobelin Stitch, Overcast Stitch, and Tent Stitch

Instructions: For Pond Bottom, cut a piece of dark blue plastic canvas 65 x 65 threads. (**Note:** Pond Bottom is not worked.) Cut remaining pieces from clear plastic canvas. Refer to photo to work Fish Fronts in colors to match Fish Backs. Follow charts and use required stitches to work remaining Fishing Set pieces. Use color to match stitching area for all joining. Thread wire lengths under Gobelin Stitches on wrong side of Pole Front. With wrong sides together, join Pole Front to Pole Back. Cut a 24" length of yellow yarn. Glue one end of yarn between magnets. Tie remaining yarn end to end of Pole and trim short end close to knot. Join Pond Sides along short edges. Join Pond Sides to Pond Bottom. For each Fish, refer to photo to place one paper clip between wrong sides of Fish Front and Fish Back. Join Fish Front to Fish Back. Refer to photo to glue moving eyes to Fish Front.

Fishing Set designed by Jack Peatman for LuvLee Designs.

NL	COLOR
00	black - 17 yds
02	Christmas red - 9 yds
23	fern - 9 yds
32	royal - 30 yds
35	sail blue - 15 yds
36	baby blue - 14 yds
38	gray - 10 yds
41	white - 16 yds
57	yellow - 14 yds
58	bright orange - 9 yds
60	bright blue - 9 yds
62	bright pink - 9 yds
64	bright purple - 9 yds
	optional color

Pond Side (65 x 21 threads) (Work 4)

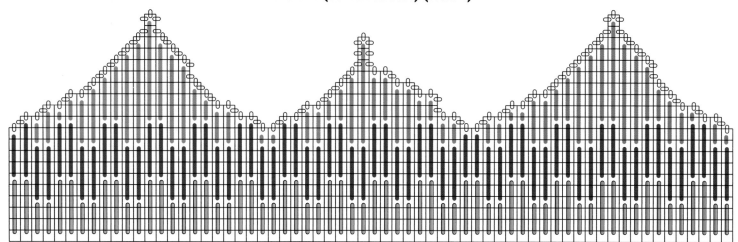

Pole Front/Back (91 x 12 threads)

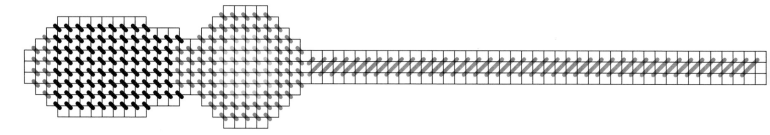

Fish Back (21 x 14 threads each)

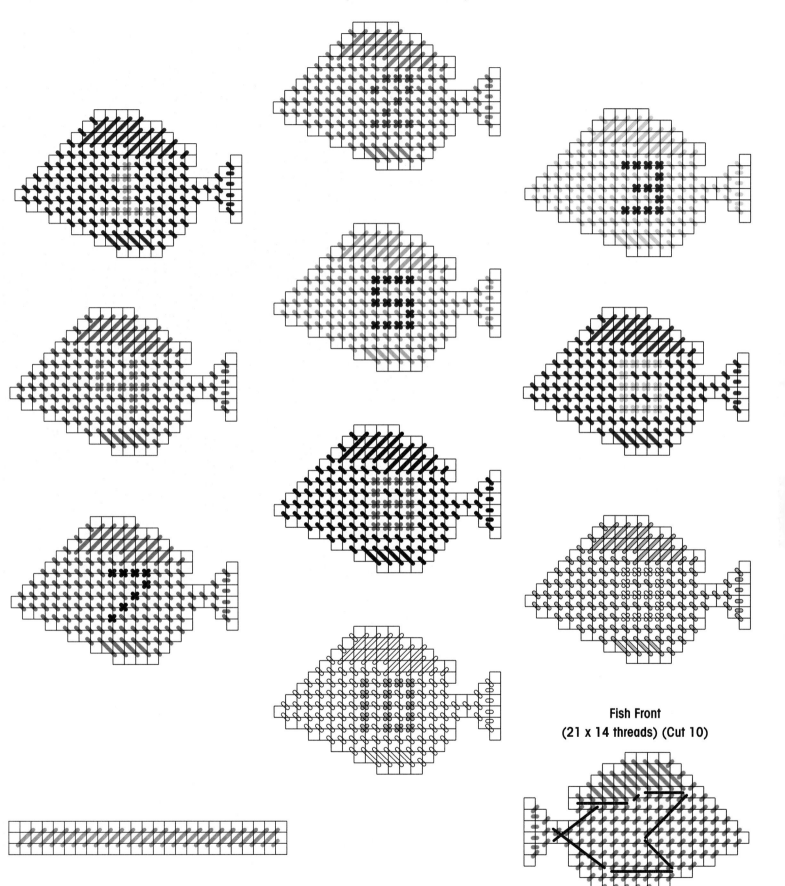

**Fish Front
(21 x 14 threads) (Cut 10)**

APPLES FOR TEACHER

Give your favorite teacher a head start on the school year with our charming classroom collection. Adorned with ABC's and 1-2-3's, the mug is letter-perfect for holding pens, pencils, or a cup of coffee, and the matching eraser cover makes cleaning the blackboard fun. This back-to-school set, complete with an apple pencil topper, is sure to make the grade!

TEACHER'S SET

Skill Level: Beginner

Supplies For Entire Set: Worsted weight yarn or Needloft® Plastic Canvas Yarn (refer to color key), one 10½" x 13½" sheet of 7 mesh plastic canvas, #16 tapestry needle, red Crafter's Pride® Stitch-A-Mug™, 5"w x 2"h chalkboard eraser, pencil, and clear-drying craft glue

Stitches Used: Backstitch, Mosaic Stitch, Overcast Stitch, and Tent Stitch

MUG INSERT

Size: 3⅜"h x 3⅛"d

Instructions: Follow chart and use required stitches to work Mug Insert. Use green to join short edges, forming a cylinder. Place Mug Insert into Stitch-a-Mug™, aligning joined edges with mug handle. Remove stitched piece before washing mug.

ERASER COVER

Size: 5"w x 2"h

Instructions: Follow chart and use required stitches to work Eraser Cover. Refer to photo to glue Eraser Cover to chalkboard eraser.

PENCIL TOPPER

Size: 1½"w x 2"h

Instructions: Follow chart and use required stitches to work Pencil Topper. Use green and match ▲'s to join ends. Slide Pencil Topper onto pencil.

Teacher's Set designed by Lucienne Woodward.

NL COLOR

⊘	00 black
⟋	02 red
⟋	05 pink
⟋	15 brown
⟋	23 lt green
⟋	29 green
⟋	37 grey
⟋	39 ecru
⟋	41 white
⊘	57 yellow

**Pencil Topper
(13 x 14 threads)**

Eraser Cover (34 x 14 threads)

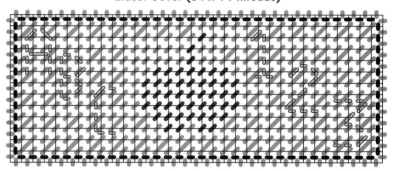

Mug Insert (64 x 23 threads)

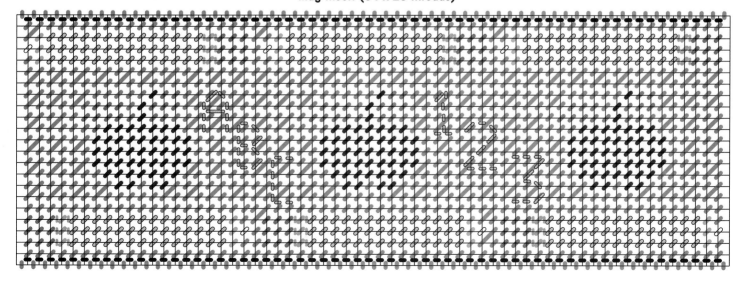

Mother's Day Tissue Box Cover

Surprise your mom on Mother's Day (or any day) with our beautiful floral tissue box cover! Designed to fit a standard-size box of tissues, its soothing colors will add a charming touch of springtime to her decor.

FLORAL TISSUE BOX COVER

Skill Level: Beginner

Size: 10"w x 3½"h x 5¼"d

(**Note:** Fits a 9½"w x 3"h x 4¾"d tissue box.)

Supplies: Worsted weight yarn or Needloft® Plastic Canvas Yarn (refer to color key), two 10½" x 13½" sheets of 7 mesh plastic canvas, and #16 tapestry needle

Stitches Used: Gobelin Stitch, Overcast Stitch, and Tent Stitch

Instructions: Follow charts and use required stitches to work Floral Tissue Box Cover pieces. Use blue for all joining. Join Long Sides to Short Sides along short edges. Join Top to Sides.

	NL COLOR		NL COLOR
✎	05 pink - 14 yds	✎	35 blue - 46 yds
◿	07 lt pink - 9 yds	✎	36 lt blue - 21 yds
✎	18 tan - 15 yds	✎	41 white - 21 yds
▨	20 yellow - 3 yds	✎	53 green - 9 yds

Short Side (35 x 23 threads) (Work 2)

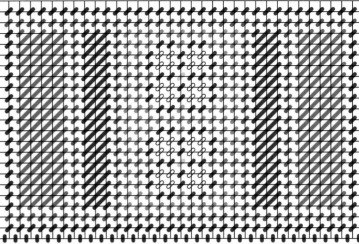

Long Side (67 x 23 threads) (Work 2)

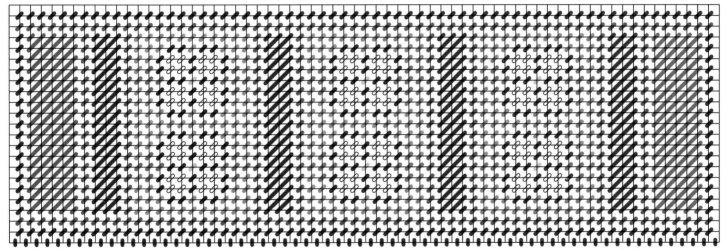

Top (67 x 35 threads)

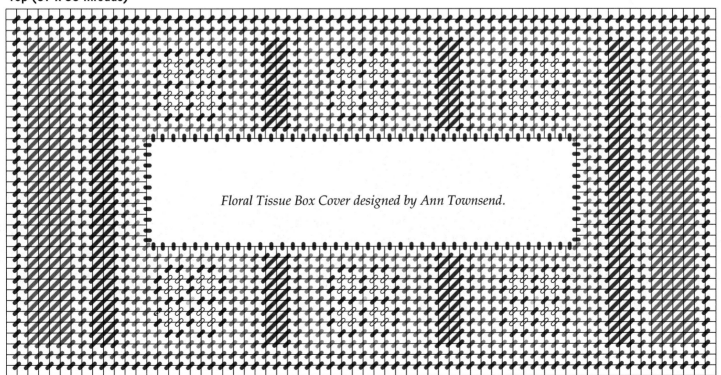

Floral Tissue Box Cover designed by Ann Townsend.

A Bunny Basket for Baby

Welcome a new arrival with this adorable bunny basket, complete with carrot handles! Filled with powder, lotion, and other newborn necessities, it's an ideal shower gift. Mom can use it later to store precious keepsakes as the baby grows.

BUNNY BASKET

Size: 9"w x 10½"h x 9½"d

Skill Level: Advanced

Supplies: Worsted weight yarn or Needloft® Plastic Canvas Yarn (refer to color keys), five 10½" x 13½" sheets of 7 mesh plastic canvas, #16 tapestry needle, 2" white pom-pom, and clear-drying craft glue

Stitches Used: Backstitch, French Knot, Gobelin Stitch, Mosaic Stitch, Overcast Stitch, and Tent Stitch

Instructions: For each Carrot Bottom, cut Carrot Top along blue cutting line and use only the lower portion of shape. Follow charts and use required stitches to work Bunny Basket pieces, leaving stitches in shaded areas unworked on Carrot Bottoms only. For Back, work Front replacing white Gobelin Stitch pattern for facial features and inner ears. With right sides up, match ■'s and work stitches in shaded areas to join Connector to Carrot Bottoms. Use color to match stitching area for all joining. Refer to photo to join Carrot Tops above ✿'s. Join Carrot Tops to Carrot Bottoms and Connector along unworked edges. Match ▲'s to tack Nose to Front. Join Front to Back above ★'s. Join Sides to Feet Back between ♦'s. Join Feet Front to Feet Back, leaving bottom edges open. Join Front and Back to Sides. For Bottom, cut a piece of plastic canvas 34 x 50 threads. (**Note:** Bottom is not worked.) Join Bottom to Front, Back, Sides, Feet Front, and Feet Back. Refer to photo to place Sides between Carrot Tops and Carrot Bottoms. Tack Carrot Tops and Carrot Bottoms to Sides. Glue Arms to Sides and Carrot Tops. Glue Flowers to Feet Front and Sides. For tail, glue pom-pom to Back.

Bunny Basket designed by Dick Martin.

NL	COLOR		NL	COLOR		NL	COLOR
00	black		25	green		55	pink
07	lt pink		26	lt green			
20	yellow		41	white			

Front/Back (42 x 70 threads)
(Cut 2, Work 1)

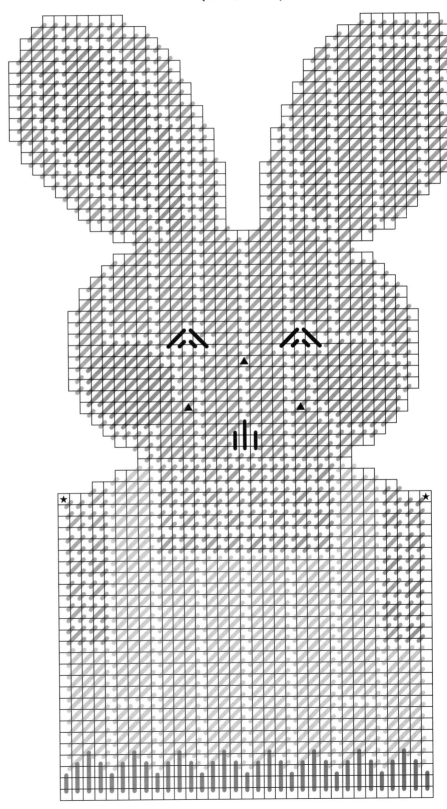

Nose (11 x 11 threads)

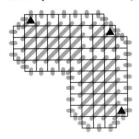

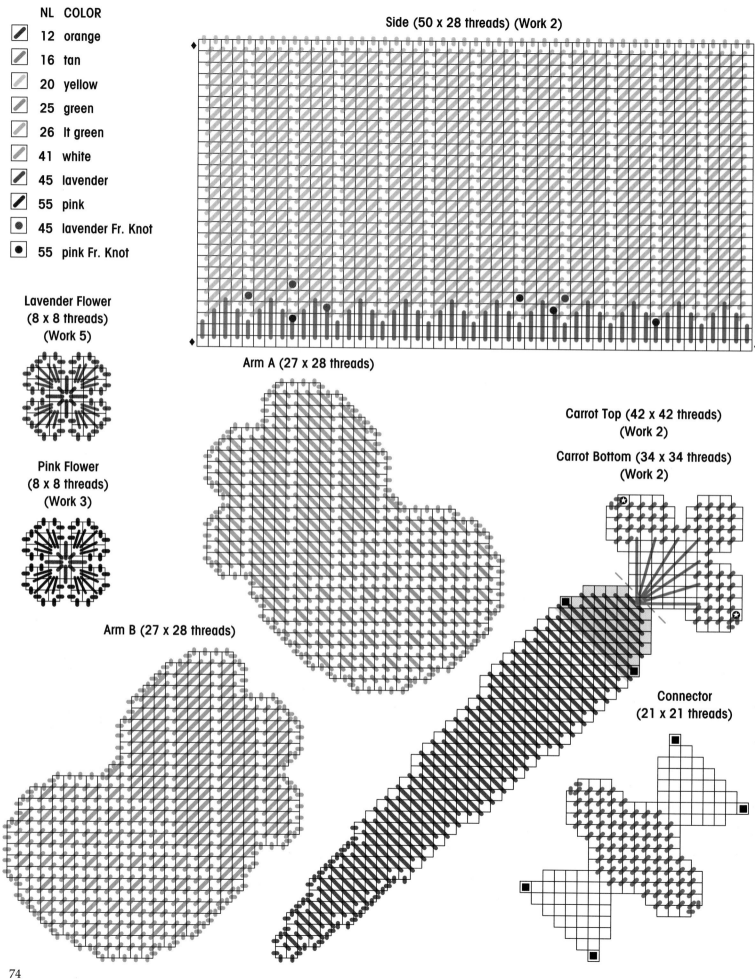

NL COLOR
12 orange
16 tan
20 yellow
25 green
26 lt green
41 white
45 lavender
55 pink
45 lavender Fr. Knot
55 pink Fr. Knot

Side (50 x 28 threads) (Work 2)

Lavender Flower
(8 x 8 threads)
(Work 5)

Pink Flower
(8 x 8 threads)
(Work 3)

Arm A (27 x 28 threads)

Arm B (27 x 28 threads)

Carrot Top (42 x 42 threads)
(Work 2)

Carrot Bottom (34 x 34 threads)
(Work 2)

Connector
(21 x 21 threads)

Feet Front (60 x 35 threads)

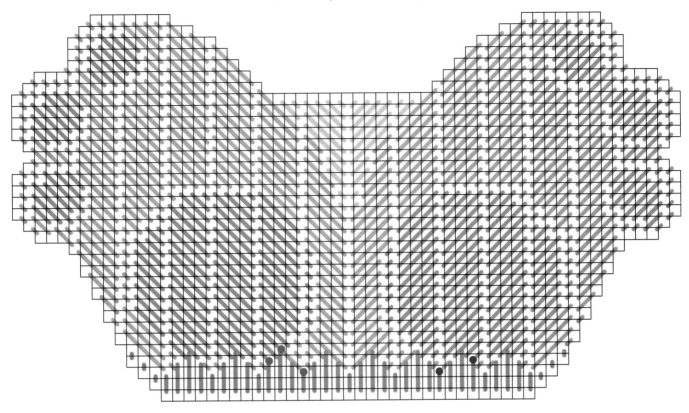

Feet Back (60 x 35 threads)

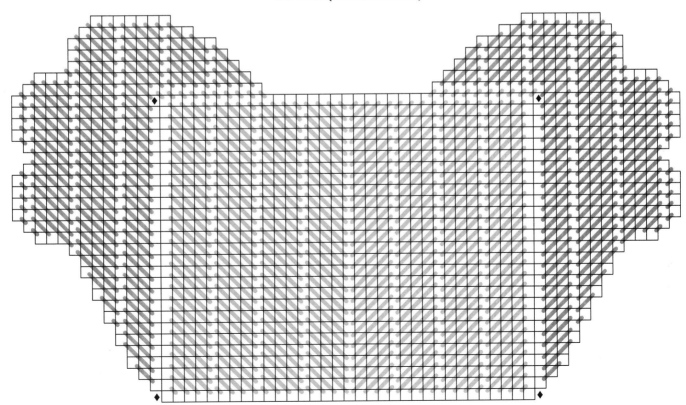

Anniversary Basket

Congratulate a special couple on their anniversary with this elegant basket. Stitched with white and gold metallic cord, it's just right for presenting a pair of goblets and a sparkling beverage. Trim the handle with a shiny bow, and your gift will really sparkle!

BASKET

Skill Level: Intermediate
Size: 8"w x 8"h x 5½"d
Supplies: Metallic gold/white cord, two 10½" x 13½" sheets of 7 mesh plastic canvas, and #16 tapestry needle
Stitches Used: Gobelin Stitch, Overcast Stitch, and Tent Stitch
Instructions: Follow chart and use required stitches to work Handle through two thicknesses. Follow charts and use required stitches to work remaining Basket pieces, leaving shaded areas unworked. Refer to photo to join Long Sides to Short Sides along short edges. For Bottom, cut a piece of plastic canvas 28 x 52 threads. (**Note:** Bottom is not worked.) Join Sides to Bottom. Match ▲'s and work stitches in shaded areas to join Rim pieces. Match ■'s to tack Handle to right sides of Long Sides. Match unworked edges to place Rim around outside of Sides and Handle. Join Rim to Sides and Handle.

Basket designed by Teal Lee Elliott.

☑ **gold/white metallic cord - 68 yds**

Short Side (28 x 24 threads) (Work 2)

Long Side (52 x 24 threads) (Work 2)

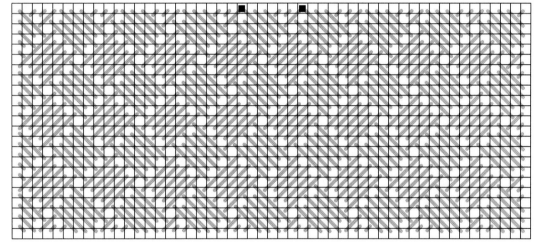

Rim (59 x 7 threads) (Work 3)

Handle (72 x 8 threads) (Cut 2)

These colorful dancing fruit magnets will give any friend's memos fresh "a-peel"! Decked out with top hats and canes, they're also cute for displaying children's artwork.

DANCING FRUIT MAGNETS

Skill Level: Beginner
Approx Size: 5"w x 5½"h
Supplies: Worsted weight yarn or Needloft® Plastic Canvas Yarn (refer to color key and photo), one 10½" x 13½" sheet of 7 mesh plastic canvas, #16 tapestry needle, magnetic strip, two 10mm moving eyes, 7mm green pom-pom, 12" length of 3mm black chenille stem, and clear-drying craft glue
Stitches Used: Backstitch, Overcast Stitch, and Tent Stitch
Instructions: Follow charts and use required stitches to work Magnet pieces.

Refer to photo to glue eyes and pom-pom to Magnet. For bow, use yarn color to match Feet. Cut an 8" length of yarn. Tie yarn in a bow and trim ends. Glue bow to Magnet. For arms and legs, cut chenille stem in half. Refer to photo to thread chenille stem through canvas. Refer to photo to glue Hands and Feet to ends of chenille stems. Shape arms and legs as desired. Refer to photo to glue Hat and Cane to Magnet. Glue magnetic strip to wrong side of Magnet.

Dancing Fruit Magnets designed by Nova Barta.

Banana (11 x 28 threads)

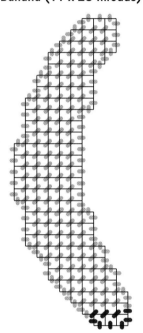

Right Hand (6 x 7 threads)

Left Hand (6 x 7 threads)

Hat (9 x 6 threads)

Right Foot (8 x 5 threads)

Left Foot (8 x 5 threads)

Cane (5 x 12 threads)

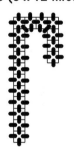

Orange (18 x 22 threads)

Apple (19 x 23 threads)

Pear (16 x 22 threads)

79

MUGS FOR MOM AND DAD

Proclaim Mom "Queen for a Day" and Dad the "King of Your Heart" with breakfast in bed and coffee served in these cute mugs. The regal cups are ideal for Mother's Day, Father's Day, birthdays, or anytime you want to give your parents the royal treatment.

MUGS

Skill Level: Beginner

Size: 3⅝"h x 3⅛" dia each

Supplies: Worsted weight yarn or Needloft® Plastic Canvas Yarn (refer to color key), one 10½" x 13½" sheet of 7 mesh plastic canvas, #16 tapestry needle, and white Crafter's Pride® Stitch-A-Mug™

Stitches Used: Backstitch, Cross Stitch, Overcast Stitch, and Tent Stitch

Instructions: Follow chart and use required stitches to work Mug Insert. Complete background with blue Tent Stitches as indicated on chart. Use blue to join short edges, forming a cylinder. Place Mug Insert into Stitch-A-Mug™, aligning joined edges with mug handle. Remove stitched piece before washing mug.

Mugs designed by Maryanne Moreck.

NL	COLOR		NL	COLOR
00	black		28	green
02	red		41	white
07	lt pink		43	brown
11	lt gold		47	flesh
12	gold		48	blue
14	dk brown		55	pink

Dad Mug Insert (64 x 24 threads)

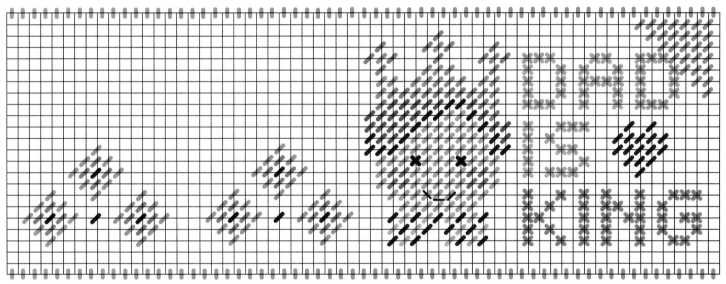

Mom Mug Insert (64 x 24 threads)

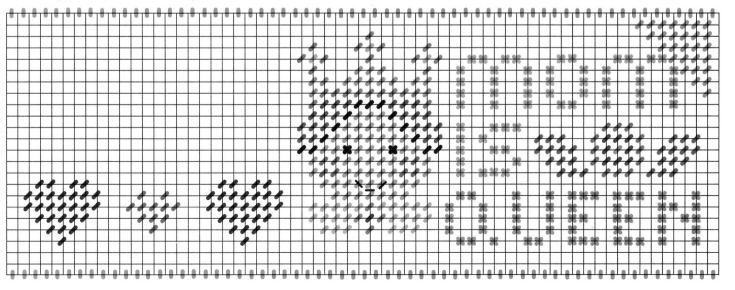

BIRTHDAY BLOSSOMS

These charming flower-of-the-month boxes are ideal for birthday gifts or any occasion. You can present your loved one's traditional birthday blossom or simply choose her favorite flower. To sweeten your surprise, tuck a little treat or trinket inside the box.

FLOWER-OF-THE-MONTH BOXES

Skill Level: Advanced

Box Size: 3¼"w x 1⅞"h x 3¼"d each

Supplies For One Box: Worsted weight yarn or Needloft® Plastic Canvas Yarn (refer to color keys), one 10½" x 13½" sheet of 7 mesh plastic canvas, and #16 tapestry needle

Stitches Used: Backstitch, Cross Stitch, French Knot, Gobelin Stitch, Overcast Stitch, Scotch Stitch Variation, and Tent Stitch

BOX

Instructions: Follow charts and use required stitches to work Flower and Box pieces, leaving stitches in shaded areas unworked. Use ecru for all joining. Join Bottom Sides along short edges. Work stitches in shaded area to join Bottom Sides to wrong side of Bottom. Join Top Sides along short edges. Work stitches in shaded area to join Top Sides to wrong sides of Top. Follow individual Flower instructions to assemble Flowers. Refer to photo to tack Flowers, Leaves, and Stems to Box Top.

JANUARY CARNATION

Instructions: Use pink for all joining. With right sides facing up, match ✗'s to join Petal B to Petal C. Refer to photo to tack Petal A pieces to center of Petal B.

FEBRUARY VIOLET

Instructions: With right sides facing up, match ✗'s to place Petal B on top of Petal A. Use purple to join Petal A to Petal B. Work a yellow French Knot at ✗.

MARCH DAFFODIL

Instructions: Use yellow to join ends of Center, forming a cylinder. With right sides facing up, match ✗'s to place Petal B on top of Petal A. Use yellow to join Petal A to Petal B. Refer to photo and use yellow to tack Center to Petals. Refer to photo and use yellow to tack Petals to Stem A.

APRIL SWEET PEA

Instructions: Refer to photo to insert Petal A into slit of Petal B. Use lt pink to tack Petal A to Petal B.

MAY LILY OF THE VALLEY

Instructions: Refer to photo and use white to tack three Petals to each Leaf.

JUNE ROSE

Instructions: Match ▲'s and use lt pink to tack Small Center to wrong side of Center at ▲'s. With right side facing out, match ✗'s and use lt pink to fold and tack Center. Refer to photo and use lt pink to shape and tack Petals to Center.

JULY LARKSPUR

Instructions: Refer to photo and use blue to tack sections of Petals together, forming a cup shape.

AUGUST GLADIOLA

Instructions: Match ✗'s and use coral to tack three Petal B pieces together, forming flower.

SEPTEMBER ASTER

Instructions: Refer to photo and use lt purple to tack Petal A, Petal B, Petal C, and Petal D pieces together.

OCTOBER CALENDULA

Instructions: Match ✗'s and ★'s to place Petal B on top of Petal C. Work stitches in shaded area to join Petal B to Petal C. Match ▲'s and ■'s to place Petal A on top of Petal B. Work stitches in shaded area to join Petal A to Petal B and Petal C through all thicknesses.

NOVEMBER MUM

Instructions: Refer to photo and use rust to tack Petals together. Refer to photo and use gold Overcast Stitches to join Center B pieces through three thicknesses. Use a gold French Knot to tack Center A to Center B pieces at ▲. Refer to photo and use gold to tack Center to Petals.

DECEMBER POINSETTIA

Instructions: Match ✗'s and use red to tack Petal A to Petal B.

Flower of the Month Boxes designed by Dick Martin.

	NL	COLOR
✦	07	pink
✦	08	lt pink
✦	23	lt green
✦	24	yellow green
✦	25	lt yellow green
✦	28	green
✦	35	blue
✦	41	white
✦	45	lt purple
✦	46	purple
✦	56	coral
✦	57	yellow

JANUARY CARNATION

Petal A
(4 x 4 threads)
(Work 3)

Petal B
(8 x 8 threads)

Petal C
(10 x 10 threads)

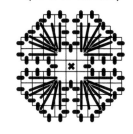

FEBRUARY VIOLET

Petal A
(5 x 5 threads)
(Work 3)

Petal B
(6 x 6 threads)
(Work 3)

Leaf
(8 x 8 threads)

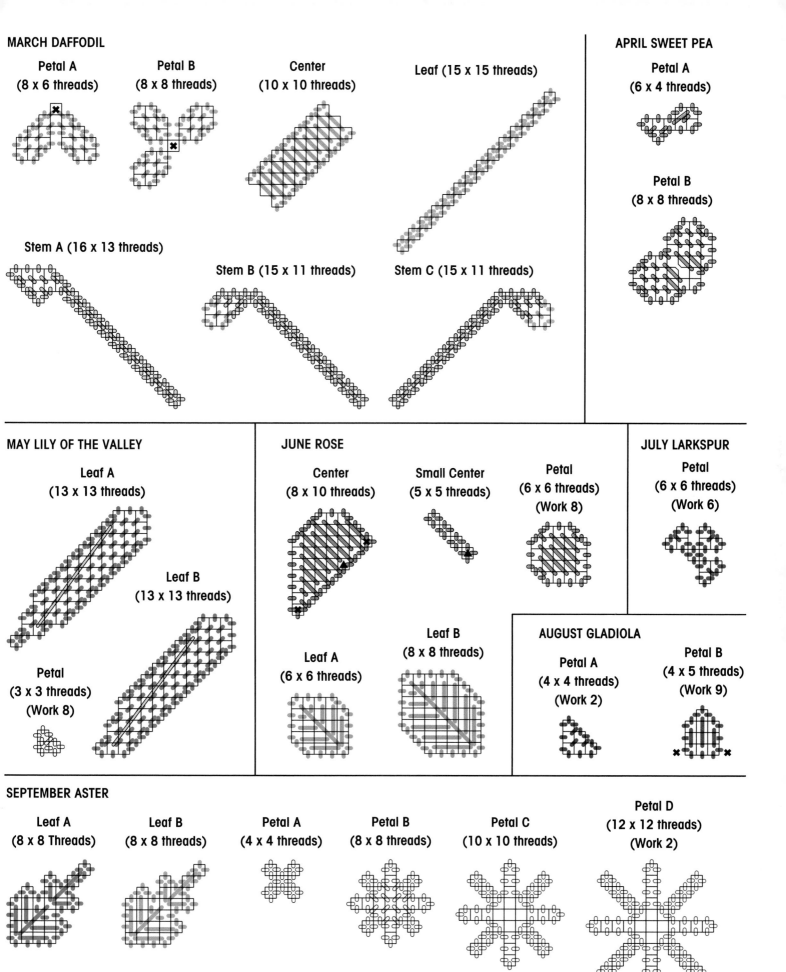

MARCH DAFFODIL

Petal A
(8 x 6 threads)

Petal B
(8 x 8 threads)

Center
(10 x 10 threads)

Leaf (15 x 15 threads)

Stem A (16 x 13 threads)

Stem B (15 x 11 threads)

Stem C (15 x 11 threads)

APRIL SWEET PEA

Petal A
(6 x 4 threads)

Petal B
(8 x 8 threads)

MAY LILY OF THE VALLEY

Leaf A
(13 x 13 threads)

Leaf B
(13 x 13 threads)

Petal
(3 x 3 threads)
(Work 8)

JUNE ROSE

Center
(8 x 10 threads)

Small Center
(5 x 5 threads)

Petal
(6 x 6 threads)
(Work 8)

Leaf A
(6 x 6 threads)

Leaf B
(8 x 8 threads)

JULY LARKSPUR

Petal
(6 x 6 threads)
(Work 6)

AUGUST GLADIOLA

Petal A
(4 x 4 threads)
(Work 2)

Petal B
(4 x 5 threads)
(Work 9)

SEPTEMBER ASTER

Leaf A
(8 x 8 Threads)

Leaf B
(8 x 8 threads)

Petal A
(4 x 4 threads)

Petal B
(8 x 8 threads)

Petal C
(10 x 10 threads)

Petal D
(12 x 12 threads)
(Work 2)

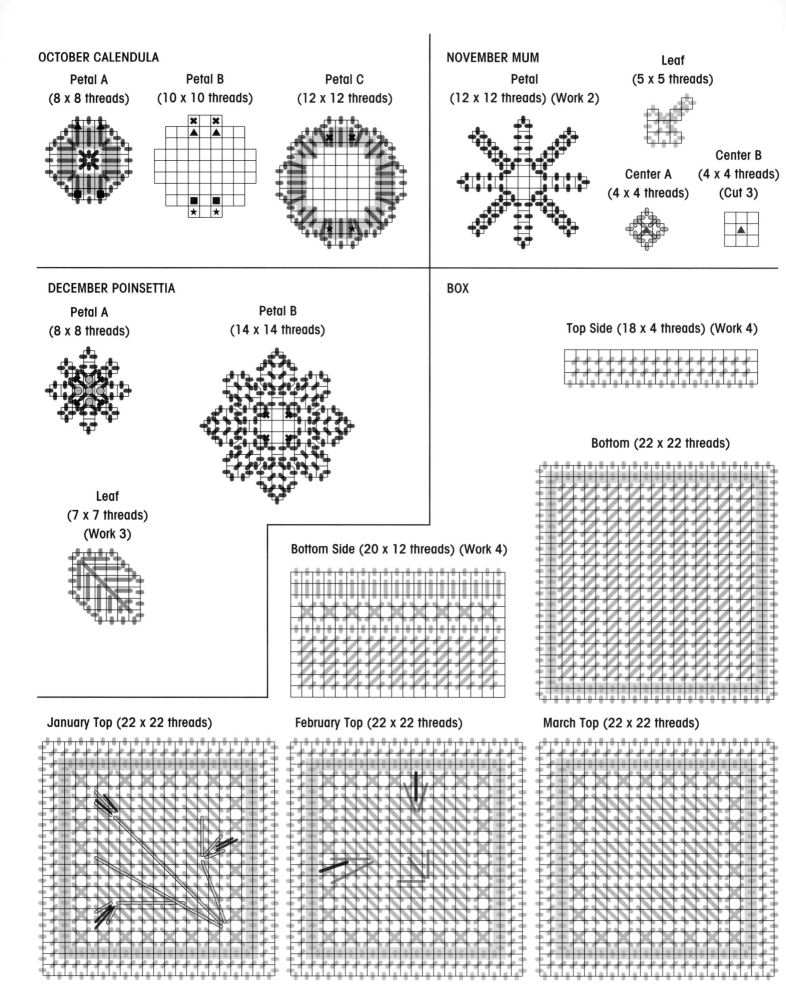

OCTOBER CALENDULA

Petal A
(8 x 8 threads)

Petal B
(10 x 10 threads)

Petal C
(12 x 12 threads)

NOVEMBER MUM

Petal
(12 x 12 threads) (Work 2)

Leaf
(5 x 5 threads)

Center A
(4 x 4 threads)

Center B
(4 x 4 threads)
(Cut 3)

DECEMBER POINSETTIA

Petal A
(8 x 8 threads)

Petal B
(14 x 14 threads)

Leaf
(7 x 7 threads)
(Work 3)

BOX

Top Side (18 x 4 threads) (Work 4)

Bottom (22 x 22 threads)

Bottom Side (20 x 12 threads) (Work 4)

January Top (22 x 22 threads)

February Top (22 x 22 threads)

March Top (22 x 22 threads)

86

NL	COLOR		NL	COLOR		NL	COLOR		NL	COLOR		NL	COLOR
02	red		10	brown		28	green		52	rust		35	blue Fr. Knot
07	pink		23	lt green		39	ecru		58	orange		57	yellow Fr. Knot
08	lt pink		24	yellow green		45	lt purple		02	red Fr. Knot			
09	gold		25	lt yellow green		46	purple						

April Top (22 x 22 threads)

May Top (22 x 22 threads)

June Top (22 x 22 threads)

July Top (22 x 22 threads)

August Top (22 x 22 threads)

September Top (22 x 22 threads)

October Top (22 x 22 threads)

November Top (22 x 22 threads)

December Top (22 x 22 threads)

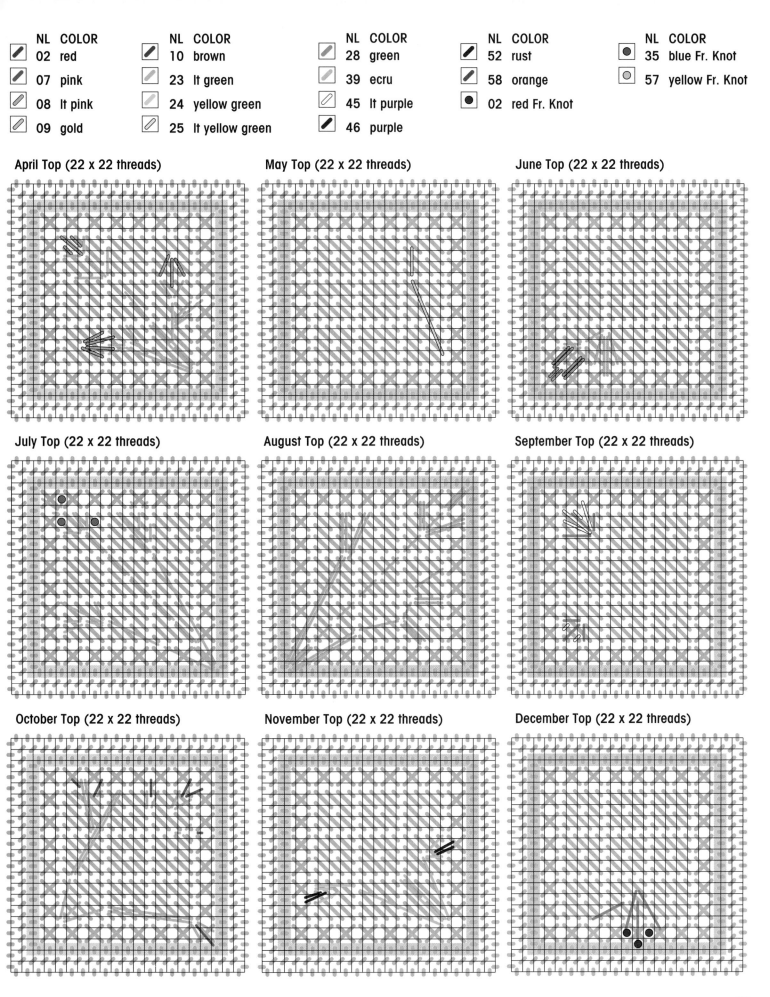

Reading Glasses Case

This reading glasses case makes a splendid gift for any occasion. Sized for the smaller glasses, it's handy for keeping spectacles scratch-free. Cross stitches and French knots provide added detail.

READING GLASSES CASE
Skill Level: Beginner
Size: 6¹/₂"w x 3¹/₈"h
Supplies: Worsted weight yarn or Needloft® Plastic Canvas Yarn (refer to color key), one 10¹/₂" x 13¹/₂" sheet of 7 mesh plastic canvas, and #16 tapestry needle
Stitches Used: Backstitch, Cross Stitch, French Knot, Gobelin Stitch, Overcast Stitch, and Tent Stitch
Instructions Follow chart and use required stitches to work Reading Glasses Case pieces. Complete background with white Tent Stitches as indicated on chart before working Backstitch and French Knots. Use blue to join Sides along unworked edges.

Reading Glasses Case designed by Ann Townsend.

NL	COLOR
07	pink - 7 yds
13	brown - 1 yd
18	lt brown - 1 yd
20	lt yellow - 4 yds

NL	COLOR
33	blue - 10 yds
34	lt blue - 7 yds
41	white - 9 yds
53	green - 2 yds

NL	COLOR
57	yellow - 5 yds
18	lt brown Fr. Knot

Side (43 x 21 threads) (Work 2)

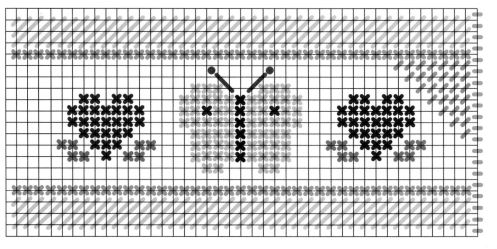

GENERAL INSTRUCTIONS

SELECTING PLASTIC CANVAS

Plastic canvas is a molded, nonwoven canvas made from clear or colored plastic. The canvas consists of "threads" and "holes." The threads aren't actually "threads" since the canvas is nonwoven, but it seems to be an accurate description of the straight lines of the canvas. The holes, as you would expect, are the spaces between the threads. The threads are often referred to in the project instructions, especially when cutting out plastic canvas pieces. The instructions for stitches will always refer to holes when explaining where to place your needle to make a stitch.

TYPES OF CANVAS

The main difference between types of plastic canvas is the mesh size. Mesh size refers to the number of holes in one inch of canvas. The most common mesh sizes are 5 mesh, 7 mesh, 10 mesh, and 14 mesh. Five mesh means that there are 5 holes in every inch of canvas. Likewise, there are 7 holes in every inch of 7 mesh canvas, 10 holes in every inch of 10 mesh canvas, and 14 holes in every inch of 14 mesh canvas. Seven mesh canvas is the most popular size for the majority of projects.

Your project supply list will tell you what size mesh you need to buy. Be sure to use the mesh size the project instructions recommend. If your project calls for 7 mesh canvas and you use 10 mesh, your finished project will be much smaller than expected. For example, say your instructions tell you to use 7 mesh canvas to make a boutique tissue box cover. You will need to cut each side 30 x 38 threads so they will measure 4½" x 5¾" each. But if you were using 10 mesh canvas your sides would only measure 3" x 3⅞"! Needless to say, your tissue box cover from 10 mesh canvas would not fit a boutique tissue box.

Most plastic canvas is made from clear plastic, but colored canvas is also available. Colored plastic is ideal when you don't want to stitch the entire background.

When buying canvas, you may find that some canvas is firm and rigid while other canvas is softer and more pliable. To decide which type of canvas is right for your project, think of how the project will be used. If you are making a box or container, you will want to use firmer canvas so that the box will be sturdy and not buckle after handling. If you are making a tissue box cover, you will not need the firmer canvas because the tissue box will support the canvas and prevent warping. Softer canvas is better for projects that require a piece of canvas to be bent before it is joined to another piece.

AMOUNT OF CANVAS

The project supply list usually tells you how much canvas you will need to complete the project. When buying your canvas, remember that several different manufacturers produce plastic canvas. Therefore, there are often slight variations in canvas, such as different thicknesses of threads or a small difference in mesh size. Because of these variations, try to buy enough canvas for your entire project at the same time and place. As a general rule, it is always better to buy too much canvas and have leftovers than to run out of canvas before you finish your project. By buying a little extra canvas, you not only allow for mistakes, but have extra canvas for practicing your stitches. Scraps of canvas are also excellent for making magnets and other small projects.

SELECTING YARN

You're probably thinking, "How do I select my yarn from the thousands of choices available?" Well, we have a few hints to help you choose the perfect yarns for your project and your budget.

To help you select colors for your projects, we have included numbers for Needloft® Plastic Canvas Yarn in our color keys. The headings in the color key are for Needloft® Yarn (**NL**) and the descriptive color name (**COLOR**). Needloft® Yarn is 100% nylon and is suitable only for 7 mesh plastic canvas.

Worsted weight yarn is used for most of the projects in this issue. Worsted weight yarn has four plies which are twisted together to form one strand. When the instructions indicate 2-ply yarn, separate the strand of yarn and stitch using only two of the four plies.

Needloft® Yarn will not easily separate. When the instructions call for "2-ply" or "1-ply" yarn, we recommend that you substitute with six strands of embroidery floss.

TYPES OF YARN

The first question to ask when choosing yarn is, "How will my project be used?" If your finished project will be handled or used a lot, such as a coaster or magnet, you will want to use a durable, washable yarn. We highly recommend acrylic or nylon yarn for plastic canvas. It can be washed repeatedly and holds up well to frequent usage and handling. If your finished project won't be handled or used frequently, such as a framed picture or a bookend, you are not limited to washable yarns.

Cost may also be a factor in your yarn selection. There again, acrylic yarn is a favorite because it is reasonably priced and comes in a wide variety of colors. However, if your project is something extra special, you may want to spend a little more on tapestry yarn or Persian wool yarn to get certain shades of color.

The types of yarns available are endless and each grouping of yarn has its own characteristics and uses. The following is a brief description of some common yarns used for plastic canvas.

Worsted Weight Yarn - This yarn may be found in acrylic, wool, wool blends, and a variety of other fiber contents. Worsted weight yarn is the most popular yarn used for 7 mesh plastic canvas because one strand covers the canvas very well. This yarn is inexpensive and comes in a wide range of colors. Worsted weight yarn has four plies which are twisted together to form one strand. When the instructions call for "2-ply" or "1-ply" yarn, you will need to separate a strand of yarn into its four plies and use only the number of plies indicated in the instructions.

Sport Weight Yarn - This yarn has four thin plies which are twisted together to form one strand. Like worsted weight yarn, sport weight yarn comes in a variety of fiber contents. The color selection in sport weight yarn is more limited than in other types of yarns. You may want to use a double strand of sport weight yarn for better coverage of your 7 mesh canvas. When you plan on doubling your yarn, remember to double the yardage called for in the instructions too. Sport weight yarn works nicely for 10 mesh canvas.

Tapestry Yarn - This is a thin wool yarn. Because tapestry yarn is available in a wider variety of colors than other yarns, it may be used when several shades of the same color are desired. For example, if you need five shades of pink to stitch a flower, you may choose tapestry yarn for a better blending of colors. Tapestry yarn is ideal for working on 10 mesh canvas. However, it is a more expensive yarn and requires two strands to cover 7 mesh canvas. Projects made with tapestry yarn cannot be washed.

Persian Wool - This is a wool yarn which is made up of three loosely twisted plies. The plies should be separated and realigned before you thread your needle. Like tapestry yarn, Persian yarn has more shades of each color from which to choose. It also has a nap similar to the nap of velvet. To determine the direction of the nap, run the yarn through your fingers. When you rub "with the nap," the yarn is smooth; but when you rub "against the nap," the yarn is rough. For smoother and prettier stitches on your project, stitching should be done "with the nap." The yarn fibers will stand out when stitching is done "against the nap." Because of the wool content, you cannot wash projects made with Persian yarn.

Pearl Cotton - Sometimes #3 pearl cotton is used on plastic canvas to give it a dressy, lacy look. It is not meant to cover 7 mesh canvas completely but to enhance it. Pearl cotton works well on 10 mesh canvas when you want your needlework to have a satiny sheen. If you cannot locate #3 pearl cotton in your area, you can substitute with twelve strands of embroidery floss.

Embroidery Floss - Occasionally embroidery floss is used to add small details such as eyes or mouths on 7 mesh canvas. Twelve strands of embroidery floss are recommended for covering 10 mesh canvas. Use six strands to cover 14 mesh canvas.

COLORS

Choosing colors can be fun, but sometimes a little difficult. Your project will tell you what yarn colors you will need. When you begin searching for the recommended colors, you may be slightly overwhelmed by the different shades of each color. Here are a few guidelines to consider when choosing your colors.

Consider where you are going to place the finished project. If the project is going in a particular room in your house, match your yarn to the room's colors.

Try not to mix very bright colors with dull colors. For example, if you're stitching a project using country colors, don't use a bright Christmas red with country blues and greens. Instead, use a maroon or country red. Likewise, if you are stitching a bright tissue box cover for a child's room, don't use country blue with bright red, yellow, and green.

Some projects require several shades of a color, such as shades of red for a Santa. Be sure your shades blend well together.

Sometimes, you may have trouble finding three or four shades of a color. If you think your project warrants the extra expense, you can usually find several shades of a color available in tapestry yarn or Persian wool yarn.

Remember, you don't have to use the colors suggested in the color key. If you find a blue tissue box cover that you really like, but your house is decorated in pink, change the colors in the tissue box cover to pink!

AMOUNTS

A handy way of estimating yardage is to make a yarn yardage estimator. Cut a one yard piece of yarn for each different stitch used in your project. For each stitch, work as many stitches as you can with the one yard length of yarn.

To use your yarn yardage estimator, count the number of stitches you were able to make, say 72 Tent Stitches. Now look at the chart for the project you want to make. Estimate the number of ecru Tent Stitches on the chart, say 150. Now divide the estimated number of ecru stitches by the actual number stitched with a yard of yarn. One hundred fifty divided by 72 is approximately two. So you will need about two yards of ecru yarn to make your project. Repeat this for all stitches and yarn colors. To allow for repairs and practice stitches, purchase extra yardage of each color. If you have yarn left over, remember that scraps of yarn are perfect for small projects such as magnets or when you need just a few inches of a particular color for another project.

In addition to purchasing an adequate amount of each color of yarn, it is also important to buy all of the yarn you need to complete your project at the same time. Yarn often varies in the amount of dye used to color the yarn. Although the variation may be slight when yarns from two different dye lots are held together, the variation is usually very apparent on a stitched piece.

SELECTING NEEDLES
TYPES OF NEEDLES

Stitching on plastic canvas should be done with a blunt needle called a tapestry needle. Tapestry needles are sized by numbers; the higher the number, the smaller the needle. The correct size needle to use depends on the canvas mesh size and the yarn thickness. The needle should be small enough to allow the threaded needle to pass through the canvas holes easily, without disturbing canvas threads. The eye of the needle should be large enough to allow yarn to be threaded easily. If the eye is too small, yarn will wear thin and may break. You will find the recommended needle size listed in the supply section of each project.

WORKING WITH PLASTIC CANVAS

Throughout this leaflet the lines of the canvas will be referred to as threads. However, they are not actually "threads" since the canvas is nonwoven. To cut plastic canvas pieces accurately, count **threads** (not **holes**) as shown in **Fig. 1**.

Fig. 1

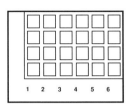

PREPARING AND CUTTING CANVAS

Before cutting out your pieces, notice the thread count of each piece on your chart. The thread count is usually located above the piece on the chart. The thread count tells you the number of threads in the width and the height of the canvas piece. Follow the thread count to cut out a rectangle the specified size. Remember to count **threads**, not **holes**. If you accidentally count holes, your piece is going to be the wrong size. Follow the chart to trim the rectangle into the desired shape.

You may want to mark the outline of the piece on your canvas before cutting it out. Use a China marker, grease pencil, or fine point permanent marker to draw the outline of your shape on the canvas. Before you begin stitching, be sure to remove all markings with a dry tissue. Any remaining markings are likely to rub off on your yarn as you stitch.

A good pair of household scissors is recommended for cutting plastic canvas. However, a craft knife is helpful when cutting a small area from the center of a larger piece of canvas. For example, a craft knife is recommended for cutting the opening out of a tissue box cover top. When using a craft knife, be sure to protect the table below your canvas. A layer of cardboard or a magazine should provide enough padding to protect your table.

When cutting canvas, be sure to cut as close to the thread as possible without cutting into the thread. If you don't cut close enough, "nubs" or "pickets" will be left on the edge of your canvas. Be sure to cut off all nubs from the canvas before you begin to stitch, because nubs will snag the yarn and are difficult to cover.

When cutting plastic canvas along a diagonal, cut through the center of each intersection. This will leave enough plastic canvas on both sides of the cut so that both pieces of canvas may be used. Diagonal corners will also snag yarn less and be easier to cover.

The charts may show slits in the plastic canvas (**Fig. 2**). To make slits, use a craft knife to cut exactly through the center of an intersection of plastic canvas threads (**Fig. 3**). Repeat for number of intersections needed. When working piece, be careful not to carry yarn across slits.

Fig. 2

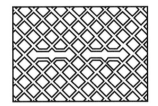

Fig. 3

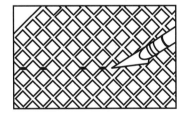

If your project has several pieces, you may want to cut them all out before you begin stitching. Keep your cut pieces in a sealable plastic bag to prevent loss.

THREADING YOUR NEEDLE

Many people wonder, "What is the best way to thread my needle?" Here are a couple of methods. Practice each one with a scrap of yarn and see what works best for you. There are also several yarn-size needle threaders available at your local craft store.

FOLD METHOD

First, sharply fold the end of yarn over your needle; then remove needle. Keeping the fold sharp, push the needle onto the yarn (**Fig. 4**).

Fig. 4

THREAD METHOD

Fold a 5" piece of sewing thread in half, forming a loop. Insert loop of thread through the eye of your needle (**Fig. 5**). Insert yarn through the loop and pull the thread back through your needle, pulling yarn through at the same time.

Fig. 5

WASHING INSTRUCTIONS

If you used washable yarn for all of your stitches, you may hand wash plastic canvas projects in warm water with a mild soap. Do not rub or scrub stitches; this will cause the yarn to fuzz. Allow your stitched piece to air dry. Do not put stitched pieces in a clothes dryer. The plastic canvas could melt in the heat of a dryer. Do not dry clean your plastic canvas. The chemicals used in dry cleaning could dissolve the plastic canvas. When piece is dry, you may need to trim the fuzz from your project with a small pair of sharp scissors.

GENERAL INFORMATION

1. **Fig. 1, page 91**, shows how to count threads accurately. Follow charts to cut out plastic canvas pieces.

2. Backstitch used for detail **(Fig. 11)** and French Knots **(Fig. 19, page 93)** are worked over completed stitches.

3. Unless otherwise indicated, Overcast Stitches **(Fig. 24, page 94)** are used to cover edges of pieces and to join pieces.

STITCH DIAGRAMS

Unless otherwise indicated, bring threaded needle up at 1 and all odd numbers and down at 2 and all even numbers.

ALICIA LACE

This series of stitches is worked in diagonal rows and forms a lacy pattern. Follow **Fig. 6** and work in one direction to cover every other diagonal row of intersections. Then work in the other direction **(Fig. 7)** to cover the remaining intersections.

Fig. 6

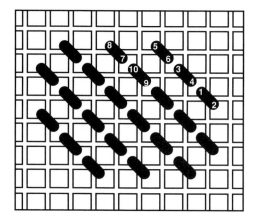

Fig. 7

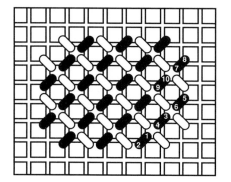

ALTERNATING MOSAIC STITCH:

This three-stitch pattern forms small alternating squares as shown in **Fig. 8**.

Fig. 8

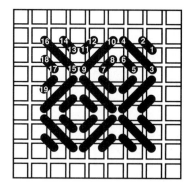

ALTERNATING OVERCAST STITCH

This stitch covers the edge of the canvas and joins pieces of canvas. With first color, work Overcast Stitches in every other hole. Then with second color, work Overcast Stitches in the remaining holes **(Fig. 9)**.

Fig. 9

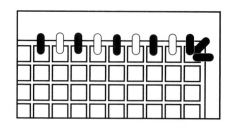

ALTERNATING SCOTCH STITCH

This Scotch Stitch variation is worked over three or more threads, forming alternating blocks **(Fig. 10)**.

Fig. 10

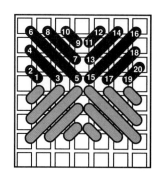

BACKSTITCH

This stitch is worked over completed stitches to outline or define **(Fig. 11)**. It is sometimes worked over more than one thread. Backstitch may also be used to cover canvas as shown in **Fig. 12**.

Fig. 11

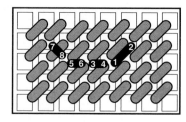

Fig. 12

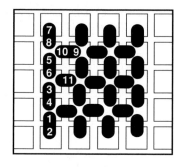

BARRED SQUARE STITCH

This stitch is composed of five Gobelin Stitches **(Fig. 13)**. The three vertical stitches are always worked on top of the two horizontal stitches.

Fig. 13

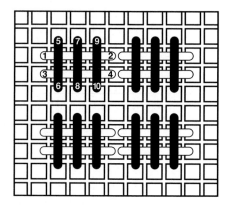

BEADED TENT STITCH

This stitch is simply a Tent Stitch with a bead slipped on the needle each time before going down at even numbers as shown in **Fig. 14**. Notice that your floss will slant up to the right just like on the chart but the beads will slant in the opposite direction (up to the left).

Fig. 14

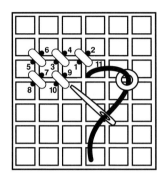

BLANKET STITCH

Bring needle up at 1, go down at 2, and come up at 3, keeping the floss below the point of the needle **(Fig. 15)**. Continue working in this manner, going in every hole at corners and every other hole on sides. Stitch going down at even numbers and coming up at odd numbers **(Fig. 16)**.

Fig. 15

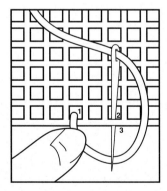

Fig. 16

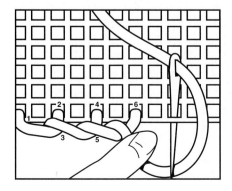

BOUND CROSS STITCH

This decorative stitch is worked over four threads and forms a bold cross **(Fig. 17)**.

Fig. 17

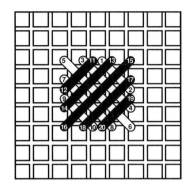

CROSS STITCH

This stitch is composed of two stitches **(Fig. 18)**. The top stitch of each cross must always be made in the same direction. The number of intersections may vary according to the chart.

Fig. 18

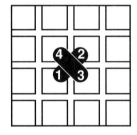

FRENCH KNOT

Bring needle up through hole. Wrap yarn once around needle and insert needle in same hole or adjacent hole, holding end of yarn with non-stitching fingers **(Fig. 19)**. Tighten knot; then pull needle through canvas, holding yarn until it must be released.

Fig. 19

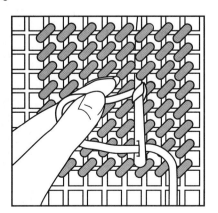

FRINGE

Fold a 12" length of yarn in half. Thread needle with loose ends of yarn. Take needle down at 1, leaving a 1" loop on top of the canvas. Come up at 2, bring needle through loop, and pull tightly **(Fig. 20)**.

Fig. 20

GOBELIN STITCH

This basic straight stitch is worked over two or more threads or intersections. The number of threads or intersections may vary according to the chart **(Fig. 21)**.

Fig. 21

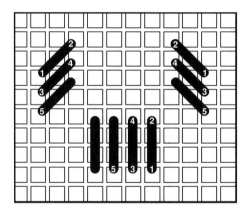

LONG-LEGGED CROSS STITCH

Like the Cross Stitch, this stitch is composed of two stitches **(Fig. 22)**. The top stitch of each cross must always be made in the same direction.

Fig. 22

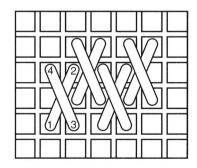

MOSAIC STITCH

This three stitch pattern forms small squares **(Fig. 23)**.

Fig. 23

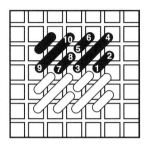

OVERCAST STITCH

This stitch covers the edge of the canvas and joins pieces of canvas **(Fig. 24)**. It may be necessary to go through the same hole more than once to get an even coverage on the edge, especially at the corners.

Fig. 24

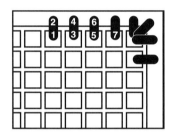

SCOTCH STITCH VARIATION

This stitch is a Scotch Stitch with a dimple in the center **(Fig. 25)**. The Scotch Stitch Variation may slant in the opposite direction.

Fig. 25

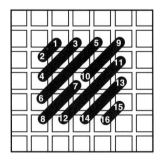

TENT STITCH

This stitch is worked in vertical or horizontal rows over one intersection as shown in **Fig. 26**. Follow **Fig. 27** to work the **Reversed Tent Stitch**.

Fig. 26

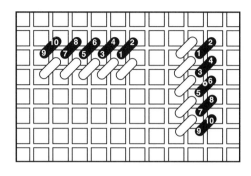

Fig. 27

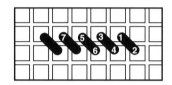

Sometimes when you are working Tent Stitches, the last stitch on the row will look "pulled" on the front of your piece when you are changing directions. To avoid this problem, leave a loop of yarn on the wrong side of the stitched piece after making the last stitch in the row. When making the first stitch in the next row, run your needle through the loop **(Fig. 28)**. Gently pull yarn until all stitches are even.

Fig. 28

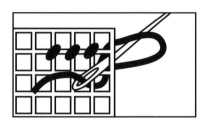

Instructions tested and photography items made by Janet Akins, Kandi Ashford, Kathleen Boyd, Virginia Cates, Sharla Dunigan, Jo Ann Forrest, Vivian Heath, Christel Shelton, and Janie Wright.

INDEX